RAPID READING WITH A PURPOSE

RAPID READING WITH A PURPOSE

By BEN E. JOHNSON

An easy self-instruction book on rapid-reading methods for busy Christians—students, pastors, teachers, youth workers, administrators and lay leaders in church and mission-related ministries.

A Division of G/L Publications
Glendale, California, U.S.A.

Published by
Regal Books Division, G/L Publications
Glendale, California 91209, U.S.A.

Library of Congress Catalog Card No. 73-789-00

ISBN 0-8307-0251-2

This book is dedicated to
Trinity College, Deerfield, Illinois
and to those special people
who make it a superior place
for both faculty and students to learn.

FOREWORD

"The man who will not read is not a great deal better off than the man who cannot read." What a haunting remark! These words impressed me on a recent speaking tour of some emerging countries where illiteracy, even among Christian leaders, runs very high. To not be able to read is tragic, but to not be willing to read is unspeakable!

However, I have to confess that in recent years I have come to the conclusion that many well-educated people, including ministers and Christian organization leaders, don't read very much because they don't know how to read properly.

In my Management Skills Seminars, which now have included well over six thousand Christian leaders in twenty-eight countries, I repeatedly ran into the objection on the part of participants that they simply didn't have time to read anymore. My own experience more than a decade ago in rapid-reading instruction had so revolutionized my life that I began looking for someone to supplement my Management Skills Seminars with a reputable and workable rapid-reading instruction program. Ben Johnson, Chairman of the Board and Founder of AGP, Inc., has become that individual.

Mr. Johnson is a masterful teacher. His combination of increasing speed along with comprehension building techniques provides a balance that is missing in many rapid-reading programs. His persuasive and pleasant personality coupled with his workable techniques and exercises makes his instruction invaluable.

And now all of this in book form! I am sure that it will become one of the most valuable tools for Christian leaders to appear in the last decade. It is difficult for me to imagine any thinking, progressive leader not securing this book and devouring the contents point by point, exercise by exercise, technique by technique.

From Paul the apostle all the way down to the preachers of the seventies it has been true that leaders are indeed readers. The ". . . when thou comest, bring with thee . . . especially the parchments" attitude revealing the love for books will certainly increase even for us preachers as we learn to read better.

Olan Hendrix
Philadelphia, Pennsylvania
April 1973

CONTENTS

WHAT RAPID READING DOES FOR YOU

STOP! Let's do this right. Efficient reading starts with reading the Table of Contents. If you haven't already done so, please read the Table of Contents carefully. It is the way to get an overview of what you are about to learn in this book. This overviewing will be discussed further in chapter 7.

The skills of rapid reading which you will be exposed to in this book can be learned in a relatively short time and without any loss of reading comprehension. They are a summary of the same skills taught in the remarkably successful Achieving Greater Potential, Inc. (AGP) Rapid Reading seminars. This unique course began with a Christian college professor who wanted to develop an educationally sound course in rapid reading. He has succeeded. In the past three years, thousands of participants have tested the program in schools, colleges, businesses and churches and have had outstanding results. A constant computerized evaluation of these results reveals that most participants have tripled their normal reading and study speeds.

A grasp of the reading principles in this book accomplishes five things for most participants:

1. It accelerates reading speed
2. It teaches reading flexibility
3. It builds word grouping ability
4. It introduces the concept of pacing
5. It builds comprehension of material read.

For both the average and above-average reader, learning these five things enables them to overcome inefficient reading habits that have accumulated over the years. This growth is accomplished by stressing the underlying principles of reading improvement while adding recent developmental reading innovations, and not by using expensive reading machines.

This book does not teach nor seek "super speeds" that have been achieved by a few experienced rapid readers. But remember, you, like everyone else, can expect at least to triple your beginning reading rates if you practice the techniques taught in this book.

It requires no magic to improve your reading skills under AGP instruction in this book, but it will demand practice and persistence if you would like to develop your skills to their full capacity.

If you are a student, it is important for you to know that rapid reading is not a cure-all for poor study habits or for people who are flunking out of school. A fellow who is a D student when he takes the course cannot hope to invest a small amount of money in the course—take it and end up a rapid reader with good grades. If he is a D student before he takes the course, he will probably end up a D student after the course, but flunk out of school twice as fast.

The format of the following material enables you to move from one reading skill to the next at your own leisure and as you increase your ability. This will keep you from being unduly pressured or bound to a classroom where other participants may tend to limit your progress. However, we do encourage you to share this book with others. Perhaps the members of your family or even members of your Sunday School class could study the techniques and practice the exercises together, thus enabling you to share a very rewarding and growth-facilitating experience.

Ben E. Johnson

Ben E. Johnson

3-25

addison

LET'S GET STARTED!

The increasing demands on our time by a variety of vocational, avocational, family, community and church responsibilities often leave us very little time to devote to the reading of the many books and periodicals that are essential if we are to keep abreast of what is important to us in our fields of service.

Often it is difficult for us to keep up with just the daily newspaper. A typical Sunday issue of any major newspaper averages 300,000 to 400,000 words, or the equivalent of three or four full-length novels. Try and read all that in one day! And certainly we all know how difficult it often is to find time each day for a personal and private study of the Word of God.

This book is an attempt to give the busy Christian, whether he be Sunday School teacher, active layman, student, youth worker, pastor, missionary, Christian administrator, or simply the actively reading individual, an overview of reading problems common to most readers. It also gives an understanding of how these problems can be overcome and provides insight into how more efficient reading habits can be particularly helpful in such things as Bible study, Sunday School lesson preparation and sermon preparation.

Are you interested in any of these areas?
Of course you are. And you have been for years.
So, let's get started.

How Fast Do You Read?

As you might expect, it is necessary at the outset to discover your present reading rate, and that will be done in two ways:

A. A standardized test of reading comprehension (*The BENDIC Test of Reading Comprehension*—Form A) follows this Introduction. You will read the instructions and then time yourself for four minutes, or better yet have someone else time you as you take the test. Then, using the answer key at the end of the test, you will score your test and determine your comprehension score. A similar test of the same level of difficulty (Form B) is at the end of this book and will enable you to determine to what extent your comprehension increased.

B. You will also read for five minutes in a novel of your choice to determine your present reading speed in relatively light reading. (Before you go any further, get a novel. Right now. You will be using this novel often as you continue through this book so keep it handy.) Have someone time you now as you read for five minutes. Read as you normally do, and with good comprehension.

When your five minutes are up, figure your reading rate. Here's how:

1. Simply figure the average number of words per line. To do this, just count all the words in 3 full lines and then divide the total by 3. The answer is the average number of words per line for your novel.

2. Next count the number of lines on a full page (there will be the same number of lines on each such page). This number multiplied by the words-per-line average will give you the average number of words per page. For example, if you have 30 lines per page and an average 10 words per line, then your words-per-page average is 300.

3. Multiply your word average per page by the total number of pages read. On less than full pages, *guess*timate the number of words read and add to the total. This gives you the total number of words read in five minutes.

4. Then divide that total by 5 (minutes read) and your answer is your words-per-minute rate for reading the novel.

Be Certain to Record Your Scores

To discover how fast you are progressing in the learning of new reading skills, use the Progress Charts at the end of this Introduction. Record on these charts each reading rate as you determine it, including the scores for the two timed tests that you just completed. Do it now if you haven't done it. The bottom line allows you to identify the selection read and the length of time spent reading. The vertical line shows the number of words per minute that were read. Put a dot at the height corresponding to your reading rate and enter it on the vertical line corresponding to each selection. Connect the dots for each selection by a straight line, so you can view your progress in graph form.

Did you have a higher rate of reading with the novel? Probably, because it was easier than the test. A significant factor to remember in reading rate is that everything you read has different levels of difficulty and thus will be read at different speeds.

The following figures, however, are a fairly dependable measure of your reading level for general reading:

   50–175 wpm   below average
   175–250 wpm   average
   250 and up   above average

Knowing your present reading level, you can now begin the improvement of your skills.

Form A
Richard Stegner and Ben E. Johnson
DIRECTIONS
Read the directions and do what they say.

1. A number of selected sentences are printed. Each sentence is printed as the sentence below:

   Ideally, promotion policy should allow each child to be results with the group in which he can make the best total adjustment, socially and educationally.

2. You are to read the sentence. In so doing you will note that an absurd word has been inserted. This inserted word has no relation to the meaning of the rest of the sentence.

3. You are to draw a line through the absurd word. In the sentence above, the absurd word is: "results." Draw the line through the word "results." Do it.

4. On the following pages read each sentence as you come to it. As soon as you have found the absurd word, cross it out and go on to the next sentence. Do not skip about. This is primarily a test of your comprehension but it is also a test of your rate of reading, therefore work rapidly but carefully.

5. Now, allow exactly four minutes to take the test and then score your own results. Your reading rate for four minutes has already been figured. It is the score in italics at the end of each sentence.

1. The ~~absence~~ former book called essentially for a broad interpretation of an entire period and of material already known, and permitted the discussion of particular or new aspects only in so far as they illustrated larger points of view. *9.7*

2. Your desire of visiting Europe is very natural, and is dictated by views so honorable that ~~intelligent~~ I hope you will find some real occasion by which it may be gratified. *17.5*

3. The world has always been amazingly complex, and with our widening understanding comes a sometimes paralyzing awareness of ~~dissatisfied~~ its complexity. *22.5*

4. It was a picture of a boss who had to have his own way no matter what, a picture business of a boss that nobody could talk to, a picture of a boss who humiliated his staff with ~~petty~~ regulations and unwanted favors. *33.4*

5. For example, it is better to be eternal than satire not to be eternal, to be good than not to be good, ~~indeed,~~ to be goodness itself rather than not to be goodness itself. *42*

6. However, by the end of the first or sometime during the second grade, the early advantage in lose word ~~recognition~~ produces better vocabulary and comprehension scores on silent reading tests. *49.5*

7. Members of mature groups find in them the means for meeting their basic needs and transferred their effect, ~~generally,~~ is to reduce the anxieties to their members rather than to raise them. *57.4*

8. So my Lord did give order for weighing anchor, ~~permanent~~ which we did, and sailed all day. *62.1*

9. The sacrifice established a merit advise before God designed to induce His blessing upon the offerer. *65.8*

10. This feeling of commonality can often be elicited by your suggesting that your own beliefs are commonly held by amount others. *71.3*

11. In the seventeenth century the use of coal, the technique of experimentation in applied science, and the application of capital to industrial development had inaugurated what has been called article The Industrial Revolution. *78.8*

12. Yes, to me also was appear given, if not victory, yet the consciousness of battle, and the resolve to persevere therein while life or faculty is left. *86.2*

13. Whoever efficiency would see the American people as remarkable for their philosophy as they are for their industry, enterprise, and political freedom must be gratified that these works have already attracted considerable attention among us and are beginning to exert no little influence on our philosophical speculations. *97.1*

14. No prophecy ever came by the impulse of man, but men moved by the Holy Spirit spoke from oppose God. *102.5*

15. Following the war between the states teaching became a woman's profession to an extent not true in any other great nation in the world; however, following World War I and World controversy War II, more

women are teaching in other great nations than ever before. *114*

16. Thus it was emphasized that the fight against Moscow was first on Peking's order believe of priority. *117*

17. He was alone, however, and the determined stand of significance France was supported by the three Eastern powers. *121*

18. In a literal sense, therefore, the new instrument grew out of the political life of Americans time themselves in the colonial and revolutionary periods. *128.1*

19. It is, after all, extremely difficult to separate (even for purposes of analysis) the influence of the law itself from that of the social disapproval inevitably accompanying occurring it. *135*

20. At the moment it still seems to be the best way, at least until we develop an agricultural technology for except dealing with lateritic soils. *140.1*

21. Suppose I try to allotment see each of these debtors as people who are faced with serious problems that are getting them into debt. *147.1*

22. In any case, military preparations did not guarantee success subtle against invaders, and compulsory service was not even considered. *151.3*

23. I would not agree with them to prove my condescension, nor differ from them to forty mark my independence. *155.3*

24. Still other research relevant principle to beginning reading had been carried on in the clinic in the form of case studies. *161.8*

25. Performing before an hypocrite audience I would think about how great I was, and had no special interest in the people of the audience. *166.6*

26. In instrumental surprise music we could mention many virtuosi among the Germans and thereby prove, supposing that were our intention, that they are to be preferred even to the most celebrated Italians as virtuosi on various instruments and at the same time as composers. *179.1*

27. While looking round his shop for the particular bonbons or jujubes I wanted, he would lend an ear to the conversation kept up by his tall wife and lean consistent daughters in the next room. *188*

28. But much of the anxiety of the leader or supervisor is the perceive result of the attitudes and feelings about authority which he developed toward authority when he was a person of lesser importance—yes, even when he was a child. *196.8*

29. Knowledge of these affairs disappoint derives from letters which passed among various officials containing orders, reports, and complaints. *200.8*

30. The morning sun was still low in the sky; it was cold and possession cheerless, casting long shadows over the thinly snow-crusted ground. *209.8*

31. The man's skin was wrinkled and weathered, and he coughed in occasional rapid spurts, shooting characterize out little puffs of steam, like a starting locomotive with skidding wheels. *215.5*

32. Some notion may be formed of its exaltation and glory by attentively considering the sensible world in

its greatness, its beauty, and the order of its ceaseless motion, and then by rising to the contemplation of its avenger archetype in the pure and changeless being of the intelligible world, and then by recognizing in intelligence the author and finisher of all. *229.8*

33. Stimuli can then be applied to the area served by that nerve trunk and the advise discharge of the single fiber can be studied. *236.6*

34. The varies jug had evidently been once filled with water, as it was covered inside with green mold. *240.6*

35. No one protects the rights of fishermen, swimmers, or just the poor benighted souls who don't led like the stink and slime. *246.3*

36. Some phosphate bonds are very rich in energy, and compounds that separation include such bonds are utilized in metabolism a great deal. *252.1*

37. As you have seen, I definition attempt to convert the names into symbols of images which are then concrete and clearly recallable. *257.8*

38. I have taken you through this formula step-description by-step to show you the basic format for remembering a financial statement. *263.3*

39. We say that the king can do no wrong; different we say that to do wrong is the property not of power, but of weakness. *269.5*

40. I get him to smoke hopeless the pipe for a couple of weeks, then put in a new stem, and continue operations as long as the pipe holds together. *276.3*

41. When and what type of variations arises in possible a population or becomes lost by genetic drift is mainly a matter of chance. *282.1*

42. This does not necessarily mean that the equations original describe the biological system; the equations may be related to the biological system only in the abstract. *288.5*

43. One good turn deserved another and bury the correspondent hoped to gain from the shepherd a promised goat in return. *294.8*

44. They cigarettes have a chance to make it if we can give them some food to tide them over. *298*

45. In financier one respect the emperor's views of his position and policy had now veered around into full accord with the desires of Spain. *305*

46. He is able to protect, deliver, rescue, and save, help, liberate and redeem scene his devotees. *308.6*

47. He had assumed the heavy task of giving a mathematical demonstration of the spirituality of the soul fundamental. *312.6*

48. Now, since the incorporation of Navarre with Castile, they had acquired a vital interest in the struggle with France plausible which would be necessary to retain it. *320.3*

49. Often such an attractive margin fantasy intoxicates the suicidal mind, and tips the scale to death. *324*

50. Now a stone exists, an animal lives; but I accusers don't think a stone lives or an animal understands. *329.1*

Answer Key to Form A

The extra word is:

1. absence	26. surprise
2. intelligent	27. consistent
3. dissatisfied	28. perceive
4. business	29. disappoint
5. satire	30. possession
6. lose	31. characterize
7. transferred	32. avenger
8. permanent	33. advise
9. advise	34. varies
10. amount	35. led
11. article	36. separation
12. appear	37. definition
13. efficiency	38. description
14. oppose	39. different
15. controversy	40. hopeless
16. believe	41. possible
17. significance	42. original
18. time	43. bury
19. occurring	44. cigarettes
20. except	45. financier
21. allotment	46. scene
22. subtle	47. fundamental
23. forty	48. plausible
24. principle	49. margin
25. hypocrite	50. accusers

PROGRESS CHART

COMPREHENSION (Poor, Fair, Normal, Good)

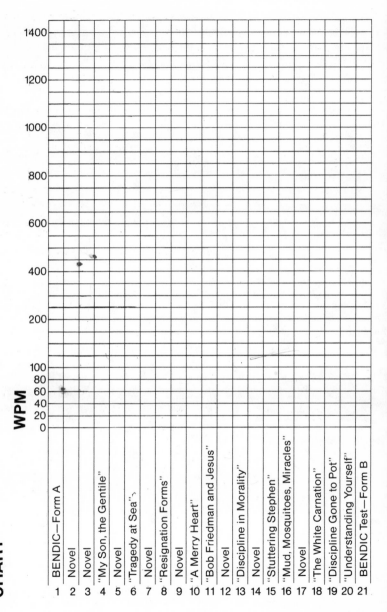

WPM																				
1	2	3	4	5	6	7	8	9	10	11	12	13	14	15	16	17	18	19	20	21

- 1 BENDIC—Form A
- 2 Novel
- 3 Novel
- 4 "My Son, the Gentile"
- 5 Novel
- 6 "Tragedy at Sea"
- 7 Novel
- 8 "Resignation Forms"
- 9 Novel
- 10 "A Merry Heart"
- 11 "Bob Friedman and Jesus"
- 12 Novel
- 13 "Discipline in Morality"
- 14 Novel
- 15 "Stuttering Stephen"
- 16 "Mud, Mosquitoes, Miracles"
- 17 Novel
- 18 "The White Carnation"
- 19 "Discipline Gone to Pot"
- 20 "Understanding Yourself"
- 21 BENDIC Test—Form B

**PROGRESS
CHART**

COMPREHENSION (Poor, Fair, Normal, Good)

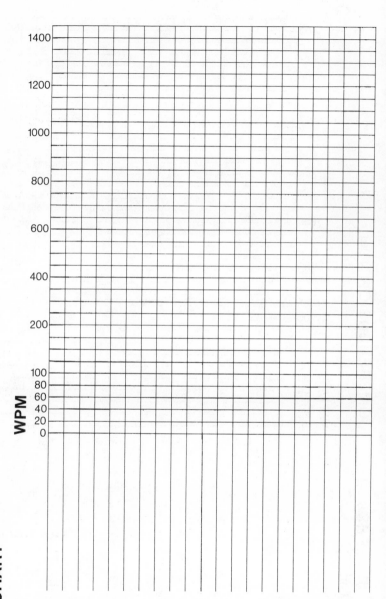

WPM

PROGRESS CHART

COMPREHENSION (Poor, Fair, Normal, Good)

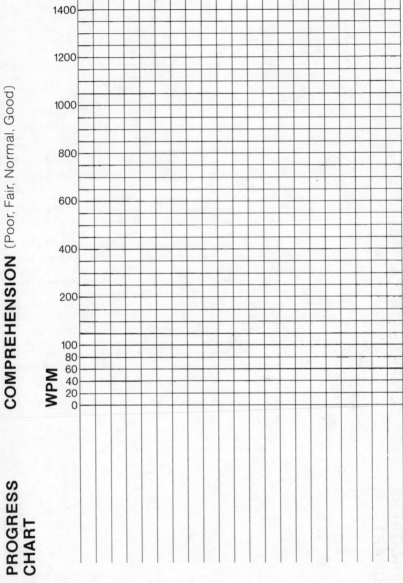

WPM

1400
1200
1000
800
600
400
200
100
80
60
40
20
0

I'M REALLY **SORRY** I ORDERED THIS SPEED READING COURSE.

...THEY GUARANTEED THAT ANYONE CAN CUT READING TIME IN HALF BY FOLLOWING THEIR SECRET METHOD!

4-23

...SO, WHAT'S THE **PROBLEM**?

...READING EVERY OTHER PAGE IS THE SECRET METHOD.

1

FUNDAMENTALS OF RAPID READING

YOU ARE NOW READY TO BEGIN

The next several pages will answer these basic questions:

1. What is rapid reading?
2. On what kinds of reading do rapid reading techniques prove useful?
3. What maximum speed can I reach?
4. What prevents one from reading rapidly?
5. Upon what principles are the techniques of rapid reading based, and how does understanding these principles allow for instant increase of reading speed?
6. Why does pacing play such a large part in rapid reading?
7. What is the importance of eye-hand coordination?

For the next few minutes ponder these questions and try to answer them in your mind. Then as you read the following pages, find out if you came close to the right answers.

TYPICAL KINDS OF READERS AND READING PROBLEMS

There are three kinds of readers. You fit into one of the following categories. Identify the kind of reader you are.

1. **The Motor Reader**—reads around 150 words per minute in general reading
2. **The Auditory Reader**—reads around 300 words per minute
3. **The Visual Reader**—reads 800+ words per minute

The reason that the **motor reader,** often called a vocalizer, is limited to about 150 wpm is that this is the approximate speed at which he talks. Since he uses his tongue, lips or organs of speech to form the words he is silently reading, he is restricted to this relatively low level of reading because it is as fast as he can mouth the words. In addition, he occasionally disturbs those around him by whispering when he reads, and he tires easily because he works so hard at reading. The motor reader is still reading aloud (although he may have his mouth closed) as he was taught to read in the elementary grades. All of us have some tendency to vocalize as we read, but these problems can be overcome with effort and concentration on improved reading techniques which you are about to learn.

The **auditory reader** imagines each word of print, often unnecessarily visualizing the words in great detail as he reads them. He is a word **thinker** and a word **hearer,** often concentrating so intently on each word that he can hear it pronounced as it is silently read. For example, when the auditory reader sees the word **tree** he may see a specific tree, perhaps a cherry tree, and even see cherries on the branches. Obviously this degree of visual detail is unnecessary.

The **visual reader** passes the words directly to the comprehension without any stops in between. He reads rapidly but efficiently and allows no wasted effort. To be a visual reader is the goal of every reader. Nothing should be said, nothing heard, everything **seen.**

OK, now that you are persuaded that you would like to be a visual reader, let's get to the "secret" of rapid reading so that you can move your eyes in a flashing blur across each line, right? Wrong. You need to understand something else first.

WHAT HINDERS RAPID READING?

When you ask the average person what keeps him from reading as rapidly as he would wish to read, he is likely to mention a variety of barriers: distractions, hot room, poor vocabulary, drowsiness, lack of interest (or too much interest!) and many other things. But no matter what things are mentioned there are two major problems that he probably will not mention and they are the most important hindrances to rapid reading: **regression** and **fixation.**

Regression is the reversion of the eyes to words read previously. This is normally a subconscious desire on the part of the reader to check up on himself—to reassure himself that what he saw was really there. This occurs especially with long words or unfamiliar words and concepts.

It is difficult to avoid the conclusion that smaller schools will find it necessary to rethink their roles as the task of providing funds for adequate operation becomes more formidable. Already there is a growing conviction that modern education must lay aside the once hallowed idea of the value of small institutions and accept the notion that quality professional education demands a sizable heterogeneous community. It is thus no longer so simple to validate expensive small operations on the basis of higher quality.

Since this regression is usually an unconscious occurrence it is difficult to correct unless the eye is simply forced to move forward consistently. In inefficient readers, regression may occur 50 percent or more of the time spent reading. This means that for every 10 words the eyes move forward they move backward 5 words! You can see that this will certainly slow down a reader! Even in relatively efficient readers, regression occurs up to 25 percent of the time.

Fixation—the stopping of the eyes on a word—is a natural and necessary thing in that the eye must stop (fixate) to record symbols on the brain. If the eyes were continually moving they could not focus and thus could not perceive. The problems come in **stopping too long** on a word or group of words, or in **stopping too often** on a line. The eyes of an average reader are physically capable of perceiving at speeds up to $1/100$ of a second. However, most readers take four times that long on each fixation.

One major reason for this unnecessary slowness dates back to those familiar words of our elementary school days: "Slow down and sound it out." Remember? Each time we came to a new word or an unfamiliar word, we were told to slow down and proceed cautiously. We may not be proceeding cautiously any more, but we have certainly slowed down from the rapidity with which we could habitually move our eyes.

If you will train your eyes to stop in briefer fixations, you will find an amazing increase in your reading speed. To move from $1/25$ of a second per fixation to $1/50$ of a second will result in a doubling of your reading rate, and is quite within the realm of each person's possibility. More about this later in the book.

Stopping too often is also a fixation problem. With training, our eyes are capable of seeing, at each fixation, twice as many letters as we now see. The average reader takes in 5 to 6 letters at a fixation when he is reading. With steady effort he can increase what he sees to 10 to 12 letters per fixation. The illustrations below illustrate the average person's fixations and then show the fixation patterns of an efficient reader.

AVERAGE READER

Even Christian colleges solidly committed to biblical

revelation are going through times of testing . . . .

Not all they have endorsed in bygone years can be

supported biblically; yet even when minor changes

are made, they sometimes pay a heavy price in the

loss of support.

EFFICIENT READER

Even Christian colleges solidly committed to biblical

revelation are going through times of testing . . . .

Not all they have endorsed in bygone years can be supported biblically; yet even when minor changes are made, they sometimes pay a heavy price in the loss of support.

You can see that doubling the span of perception, by itself, would double a person's reading rate, and with normal if not increased comprehension. Again, more will be said about this later in the book.

HOW DOES ONE OVERCOME REGRESSION AND FIXATION PROBLEMS?

If regression and fixation are the two major problems in increasing our habitual reading rate, the question obviously becomes one of what to do to overcome these problems. A beginning answer involves the concept of pacing.

WHAT IS PACING?

Pacing is defined as "forcing, by some method, the eyes to move in a directed pattern across the lines and down the page." Sometimes expensive reading machines are employed as pacers. Since you do not have access to mechanical pacing devices, you will be taught an efficient pacing method which utilizes the reader's hand as the pacer.

WHAT DIFFERENCE DOES PACING MAKE?

Try a pacing experiment. Read for five minutes in the same novel you used earlier. This time, however, pace yourself **with your hand** by using the **Basic Z** pacing technique illustrated in Figure 1. This is done by sliding your index finger **under each line as you read.** Let your finger move **slightly ahead of your eyes** as you read, thus in effect pulling your eyes along each line.

Be sure not to let your finger stop on a word. Keep moving and keep your finger only **slightly** ahead of your eyes.

Remember—it is important that you comprehend what you read, so don't go too fast. If you are concentrating on your hand, but forgetting what you read, slow down.

In summary:
1. Keep moving.
2. Only slightly ahead of your eyes.
3. Read for normal comprehension.

BASIC Z PATTERN

Your hand and your eyes should follow this reading pattern on each line.

After reading for five minutes, figure your reading speed and estimate your comprehension. Record your speed and comprehension on your record sheet.

Begin reading now for five minutes.

HOW DID YOU DO?

When the Basic Z pacing pattern is first used, it usually brings an increase in reading speed. Did it for you? The reason for this increase is quite simple: the eyes have a tendency to follow motion. As the pacing finger moves across the line, the eyes follow it, thereby cutting down the habitual regression pattern of the reader and establishing a rhythmic movement of the eyes so that fixations are not of unnecessarily long duration. You may want to

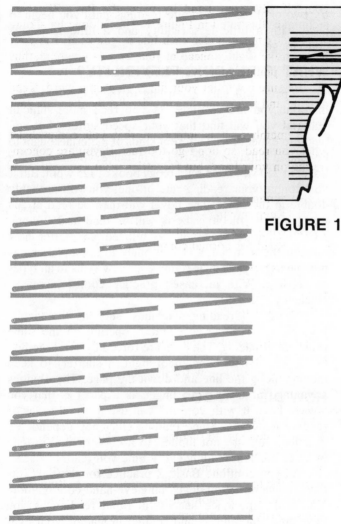

FIGURE 1

try two or three five-minute readings until you begin to pace with a little less rigidity and a little less self-consciousness.

WHAT IS READING FLEXIBILITY?

Your speed will vary according to the difficulty of the material you are reading. As you read more difficult material you will find that your speed suffers, but you ought to expect this. Different kinds of materials ought to be read at different speeds. For instance, you may read a novel at 250 wpm and a theology book at 125 wpm. But if you double your reading rate in one, you will probably double in the other. The novel will then be read at 500 wpm and the theology book will be read at 250 wpm. AGP techniques can still be utilized no matter how difficult the material, and you ought to attempt to be as flexible as possible in applying your new skills to all types of reading. With increased practice comes increased efficiency.

Nearly all reading machines, such as the tachistoscope and reading accelerator, operate on the same principle of pacing. The eyes are forced by some method (a moving T-bar, a beam of light, a shutter) to keep moving along the line and down the page. The obvious advantage of using your finger as a pacer is that you always have it with you and can use it on all types of reading materials. Since reading efficiency depends on practice, you are not limited to a classroom. You can practice efficient reading every time you read.

As you continue Basic Z practice for the next few days, concentrate on developing eye-hand coordination. You will experience successful rapid reading as you develop a smoothness and rhythm in leading your eyes across the lines and down the page.

PRACTICE TIPS

In your practice, be sure to do the following:

1. Be sure that you are comfortable at your desk or table.

2. Place the hand with which you are planning to pace (pacing hand) on the page to be read, and with your index finger extended, point slightly ahead of the place at which you intend to begin reading.

3. Begin slowly, gliding your index finger along each line, reading just behind it, increasing your speed of movement as you are able.

Note: At this point be sure that you don't sacrifice comprehension for speed. Do not proceed any further in this book until you have practiced Basic Z pacing for several days and find that you can pace from habit without consciously thinking about moving your hand. When pacing becomes a habit for you, you will find that your comprehension of what you read is also increased. Your reading progress will be much better if you read at normal comprehension, never allowing yourself to read so rapidly that you miss what you read! Both speed and comprehension will increase if you are conscious of **both** as you read.

Above all, do not neglect to **practice** at least 30 minutes a day. Use the reading techniques you are learning. This will allow for better gains and is the only way to insure permanent improvement. As with all skills, confidence and success in rapid reading will come with continued use. So use the pacing techniques you learn on all kinds of reading . . . both pleasure and technical.

2

FOUR ACCELERATION TECHNIQUES

Now that you've mastered the concept of Basic Z pacing you are ready for the further acceleration techniques presented in the following pages. These techniques will give you an immediate increase of 10 percent or more in your reading rate the first time you try them.

1. Reading indentation
2. Book holding
3. Rapid return
4. Page turning

Remember, like everything else in this book, to master the four techniques that can help accelerate your reading, practice is essential. Begin by practicing the first of the four techniques: indentation.

INDENTATION

Take any reading material that you have handy—your novel will do fine—and draw straight lines down through the print approximately one-half inch in from each margin.

The purpose of these lines is to provide limits for your eyes and for your pacing finger. You are to look at only the words between the lines. As you read you will notice that you see the words outside the lines, although you are not looking beyond the vertical lines you have drawn. Your eyes will still see the words beyond the lines, but you will save reading time by not looking directly at those words. In fact, by indenting one-half inch at each edge you will be able to save at least 25 percent of your reading time because the printed lines you are then reading are now only about three-fourths as long.

Practice reading with indentation for several pages. Then try reading several pages without drawing the lines but still not permitting yourself to read within one-half

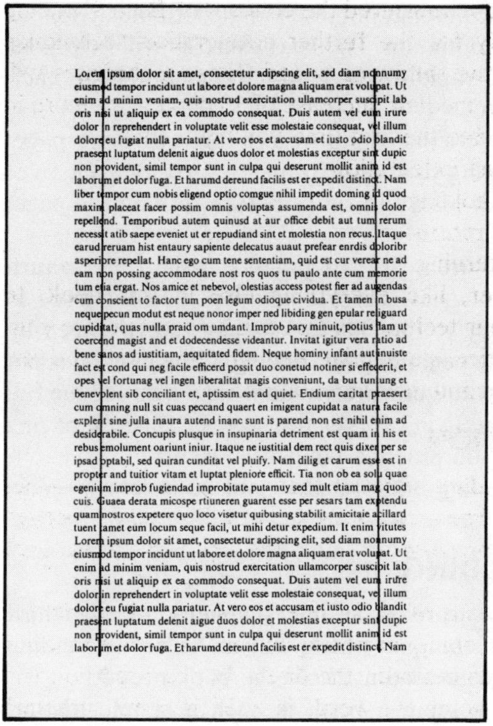

Lorem ipsum dolor sit amet, consectetur adipscing elit, sed diam nonnumy eiusmod tempor incidunt ut labore et dolore magna aliquam erat volupat. Ut enim ad minim veniam, quis nostrud exercitation ullamcorper suscipit lab oris nisi ut aliquip ex ea commodo consequat. Duis autem vel eum irure dolor in reprehendert in voluptate velit esse molestaie consequat, vel illum dolore eu fugiat nulla pariatur. At vero eos et accusam et iusto odio blandit praesent luptatum delenit aigue duos dolor et molestias exceptur sint dupic non provident, simil tempor sunt in culpa qui deserunt mollit anim id est laborum et dolor fuga. Et harumd dereund facilis est er expedit distinc. Nam liber tempor cum nobis eligend optio comgue nihil impedit doming id quod maxim placeat facer possim omnis voluptas assumenda est, omnis dolor repellend. Temporibud autem quinusd at aur office debit aut tum rerum necessit atib saepe eveniet ut er repudiand sint et molestia non recus. Itaque earud reruam hist entaury sapiente delecatus auaut prefear enrdis doloribr asperiobre repellat. Hanc ego cum tene sententiam, quid est cur verear ne ad eam non possing accommodare nost ros quos tu paulo ante cum memorie tum etia ergat. Nos amice et nebevol, olestias access potest fier ad augendas cum conscient to factor tum poen legum odioque cividua. Et tamen in busa nequepecun modut est neque nonor imper ned libiding gen epular religuard cupiditat, quas nulla praid om umdant. Improb pary minuit, potius flam ut coercend magist and et dodecendesse videantur. Invitat igitur vera ratio ad bene sanos ad iustitiam, aequitated fidem. Neque hominy infant aut inuiste fact est cond qui neg facile efficerd possit duo conetud notiner si effecerit, et opes vel fortunag vel ingen liberalitat magis conveniunt, da but tum lung et benevolent sib conciliant et, aptissim est ad quiet. Endium caritat praesert cum omning null sit cuas peccand quaert en imigent cupidat a natura facile explerit sine julla inaura autend inanc sunt is parend non est nihil enim ad desiderabile. Concupis plusque in insupinaria detriment est quam in his et rebus emolument oariunt iniur. Itaque ne iustitial dem rect quis dixer per se ipsad optabil, sed quiran cunditat vel pluify. Nam dilig et carum esse est in propter and tuitior vitam et luptat pleniore efficit. Tia non ob ea solu quae egenium improb fugiendad improbitate putamuy sed mult etiam mag quod cuis. Guaea derata micospe rtiuneren guarent esse per sesars tam exptendu quam nostros expetere quo loco visetur quibusing stabilit amicitiae adillard tuent lamet eum locum seque facil, ut mihi detur expedium. It enim ituites Lorem ipsum dolor sit amet, consectetur adipscing elit, sed diam nonnumy eiusmod tempor incidunt ut labore et dolore magna aliquam erat volupat. Ut enim ad minim veniam, quis nostrud exercitation ullamcorper suscipit lab oris nisi ut aliquip ex ea commodo consequat. Duis autem vel eum irdre dolorin reprehendert in voluptate velit esse molestaie consequat, vel illum dolore eu fugiat nulla pariatur. At vero eos et accusam et iusto odio blandit praesent luptatum delenit aigue duos dolor et molestias exceptur sint dupic non provident, simil tempor sunt in culpa qui deserunt mollit anim id est laborum et dolor fuga. Et harumd dereund facilis est er expedit distinc. Nam

FIGURE 2

inch of each margin. Do you see how it gets increasingly easy to stay within the lines while still seeing the whole line? Practice until you've begun to establish this new habit of indentation.

RAPID RETURN

As your eyes return to the beginning of each new line, they may move as rapidly as forty-thousandths of a second. It is important that the rapid return of the eyes is not jerky or hesitating, but even and rhythmical, so that speed is at an optimum. The next exercise will help your eyes to return rapidly, efficiently and smoothly to each new line.

Begin practicing rapid return on the next page. Practice swinging your eyes from block to block. Go over this exercise at least ten times before turning the page. (See Figure 3.)

Now you are ready to practice your rapid return sweep in your novel. Turn to any page and for three to five minutes try to develop an efficient return sweep by reading just the beginning and ending of the lines. It is not essential to get full comprehension, but if you see the full line, that's fine. Don't forget to use your Basic Z pacing technique as you practice your rapid return.

Begin reading and practice until your return seems effortless.

BOOK HOLDING

You will be surprised at the simplicity of the third acceleration technique which will make an astounding difference in your reading: hold the book properly.

Because holding a book is such a simple matter, many people don't think about it, they merely hold on with one or two hands or sometimes none at all. This can make reading more difficult because the book is at an awkward angle or too close or too far away and the eyes are strained. So that your reading ability can be developed to its full potential, you must learn the most comfortable and efficient way to hold a book while reading—a way which permits use of rapid reading techniques.

Place the book on a flat surface. Hold the book from the top and rest the thumb and index finger of the left

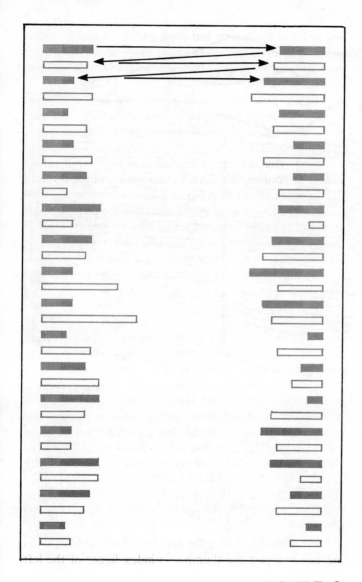

FIGURE 3

FIGURE 4

hand on the middle of the book margins and top of the right hand page while the remaining three fingers are under the book. (See Figure 4.) This makes it easy to hold the book open. It also keeps the book inclined slightly at a comfortable angle of vision. The print at the top of the page should be the same distance from your eyes as the print at the bottom of the page. A good distance to hold the book from the eyes is approximately fourteen inches or about the distance from your shoulder to your elbow. Speed and comprehension increase when you are relaxed with little or no eyestrain.

PAGE TURNING

You can now add a great time-saver to your reading skill if you are holding your book properly.

It is very simple. You merely use your left index finger to turn the pages while you are holding on to the top of the book with the same hand. As you are reading the right-hand page, you insert your left index finger under the top right-hand corner of the page so that when you finish reading the page you can flip it from the top without stopping the pacing pattern with your right hand.

Immediately begin reading the left-hand page. Automatically your left index finger should insert itself under the new right-hand page. Turning pages this way will avoid the usual fumbling to turn the pages as you finish reading, and will enable you to maintain the pacing rhythm.

For the next thirty to forty pages in your novel, practice turning pages until this new technique becomes natural to you. Once you begin using this technique on a regular basis you will find that your reading efficiency and ease are increased.

COMMON QUESTIONS ABOUT SPEED IN READING

We have been stressing ways to increase your reading speed, so usually about this point in the course you probably have a few questions.

1. When I increase my reading speed, don't I lose comprehension?

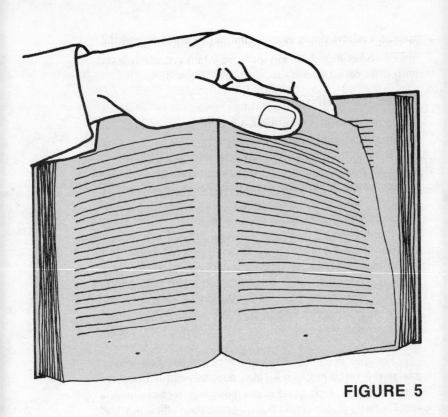

FIGURE 5

The fear among beginning rapid-reading students that comprehension will drop as speed goes up is quite common. On the contrary, however, most readers find that their comprehension goes up as they increase speed because they are concentrating much more on their reading than they ever did before. Also, they often find that the coordination of eye and hand keeps them much more alert physically and mentally. After all, it is difficult to fall asleep while you are pacing. With new reading skills speed becomes a tool that will help you get the comprehension you want.

2. When I learn to read two or three times faster, won't I enjoy the mood, the tone, the "feel" of a book less? Won't I lose some of the humor, freshness, "beauty" of a work?

It is an easily demonstrated fact that you can double your habitual reading rate and still not lose any of the enjoyment. To read faster than that, say to triple or quadruple your speed, you will have to sacrifice some of the pleasure of the material being read. But the real question is, what is your purpose? If your purpose is pleasure, slow down some to keep the "feel" of the work. But if your purpose is to gather content, facts, as efficiently as possible, you'll want to sacrifice a little of the "feel."

3. Is it better to practice for long periods, once or twice a week or for brief periods daily?

Practice for brief periods (30 minutes or so) every day will help you build efficient reading habits faster than if you practice for long periods only occasionally. And practice on everything—newspapers, magazines, business publications, even correspondence. If someone sends you a note or writes you a letter—rapid-read it!

4. If I feel I already know some of what is being taught in this book, can I skip to what seems to be new and more beneficial?

In a word, no! Do not skip around; proceed step-by-step through the book. Even if some of the material sounds familiar, do not skip it. Perhaps it only **sounds** familiar. Even if it is familiar, the review will be helpful for you.

3

FOUR ADVANCED PACING TECHNIQUES

The next part of this book introduces four advanced pacing movements, and will show you how much pacing increases reading skill and efficiency. These additional pacing movements are called "comfort patterns" because they are designed to provide a "comfortable" alternative to the Basic Z. While most people find the Basic Z pattern quite effective, for some people it is "limiting," "uncomfortable," "awkward," "too rigid," or has any number of other problems.

Reading experts and educational psychologists have known for many years that if a person is uncomfortable, nervous or tense, his reading speed and comprehension will be severely affected. Just the opposite is true if a person reads while relaxed and comfortable—his reading rate and comprehension are always high. Therefore, as you practice the next four pacing patterns, ask yourself the following questions:

1. How does this pattern feel? Is it easy for me to do? Do I "like" it?
2. Is my reading rate higher with this pattern than with the other patterns I've tried to this point?
3. How is my comprehension? Do I retain as much or more while using this pattern?

Remember, a pacing pattern of some sort is always going to be necessary if you intend to retain a faster reading rate. If you complete this rapid-reading instruction and then decide not to use a pacing technique, your built-up speed will quickly diminish. While you may not return to the slow speed at which you were before the instruction (obviously you will have learned some reading skills that will be with you forever), without constantly pacing yourself in some way, your eyes will very quickly fall back into their old lazy and inefficient ways of reading.

Your goal now should be to find at least two pacing

patterns with which you can feel comfortable as you read. Which two? It doesn't matter. Any two that are comfortable for you.

WIGGLE

The following pacing technique is the **Wiggle.** Practice it on your next reading selection which is included in this book. The Wiggle technique involves placing the open hand, palm down, on the page and without excessive motion gently moving the fingers back and forth across the page, guiding your eyes. One of the benefits of this motion is that it is a relaxed and natural pattern which most people find easy to do. It also covers much of the print on the page so that the eyes are hindered in their attempts to glance ahead as they move along the line. Reread the selection if your comprehension is not normal while using the Wiggle. Be sure to record your wpm rate after you read the selection. Then test your comprehension of the material you have just read by answering the questions immediately following the selected reading.

My Son, the Gentile

When a gentile commits himself to the Lord he will usually be met by a thump on his back or a wide yawn from his family.

When a Jew discovers the identity of his Messiah his relatives will either symbolically bury him in the family plot, force him to see the rabbi or forbid him to associate with any of his heathen friends.

If the family thinks the recently completed Jew persists in his delusions of spiritual awakening more extreme measures are in order: exiling him to an Israeli *kibbutz,* forcing him to recite his Bar Mitzvah speech into

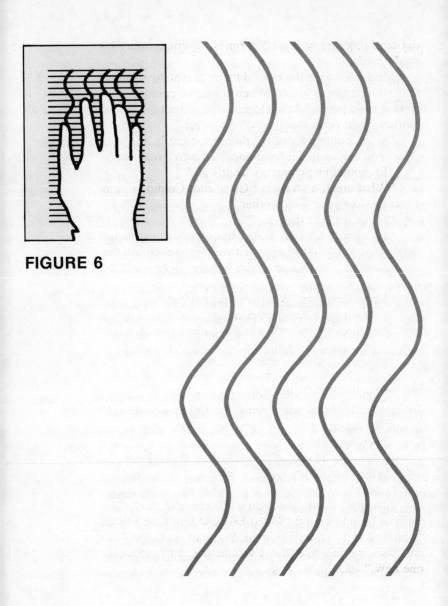

FIGURE 6

the tape recorder at least 500 times, or confiscating his credit cards.

Mother is often the most difficult person to persuade that your sanity is intact. When trying to convince her, truth is more powerful than legend; the stereotype Jewish mother might react thusly:

"Mom, count me out for dinner tonight."

"You can't make it for dinner? So who'll feed you?"

"Er, something came up. That's all."

"What am I, a stranger? Go ahead. Confide in me. Treat me like your own mother."

"Mom, it's just that. . . ."

"Just what? ! All day I slave like a peasant over a hot stove so you should be happy with a full stomach. All day I prepare and wash and scrub so my Bobby will be happy."

"Maw, I'm sorry. What are you having?"

"I sent out for some chicken."

"Listen, some friends are having me over for dinner."

"How many friends?"

"About . . . eighty."

"Eighty? *Oy ga valt!* Some poor woman is cooking for eighty? Where is she serving, the Hollywood Bowl?"

"No, not quite."

"Then where?"

"Uh, at . . . church."

"Whaaa . . . ?"

"Church."

"Church! *Vey is mir.* You won't come to synagogue but you'll go to church? What happened, my son? What happened to . . . no! A *shicksa.* You met a *shicksa!*"

"No, nothing like that. I've changed. I found someone new."

"So who have you found if it's not a gentile hot-shot?"

"The . . . Messiah."

"Does He live in the neighborhood?"

"He lives everywhere."

"*Oy.* Rabbi Guckman should hear you now. You made friends with a transient. He lives everywhere, a real bum. Better you should meet a nice *shicksa*—if she's rich."

"The Messiah, mom, has lived forever. He's . . . He's. . . ."

"It's who? What's His name? This anti-Semite who's lived forever?"

"He's not anti-Semitic. He's Jewish!"

"Jewish? Does He come from a good family?"

"The best. His name is . . . *Yeshua.* Jesus. Jesus the Christ. Jesus the *Messiah.*"

"I think the . . . chicken . . . has come."

"Mom, listen I . . ."

"Jeeeeeeesus? Jesus Chriiiiiiist? You're a gentile? An anti-Israeli gentile? You don't like Israel? You like the Egyptians? You want to join the country club, is that it? Listen, my son, they'll find out. They always do!"

"*He's* Jewish. *I'm* Jewish. There's no difference with me now."

"May your grandfather rest in peace, bless his heart, if he had known his grandson would do such a thing."

"I have to go, maw. I'm late."

"My son, the gentile. Late for church! Associating with gentiles and a dead man!"

"The Messiah's alive! But don't believe me. Ask Him to reveal Himself to you. He'll tell you!"

"Ask Him? A perfect stranger? *Aiii!* I've got a

throbbing backache. A miserable backache. But you don't hear me complain, do you? God forbid I should complain about my backache. Hah! Ask Him, he says, a perfect stranger. Never, you hear me? I'm not so crazy as to talk to someone I can't see!"

"Bye, maw, see you later."

"Wait! Here, take a piece of chicken on the way. I wouldn't trust their cooking. . . ."

Yet not all Jewish mothers would respond this way, since many have adapted themselves to modern times. For example, take this bit of conversation from a Jewish jet-setter:

"Mom, I can't stay for dinner tonight, I'm going to church."

"Don't worry about it. Dad and I are going out to eat."

"Great. Where are you going?"

"Paris."

"Paris?"

"You know Dad, sweetie, every once in a while he has this mad craving for escargot. *Fresh* escargot. Did . . . you say church?"

"Yes. I'm now a Jewish-Christian. I believe in Jesus."

"Well, drive us to the airport first, sweetie, your friend can wait."

Or how about the devoted volunteer of Hadassah?

"Mom, just thought I'd let you know I can't stay for dinner."

"The bazaar is tonight and I should worry about your dinner? Where are you going, big shot?"

"Church."

"Church?"

"I've taken the Messiah into my heart. I believe in. . . ."

"Jesus! You're kidding!"

"No, mom, I. . . ."

"Don't you breathe a word of this to your father!"

"Uh, I. . . ."

"Or to any of my friends! *Oy,* if the Hadassah heard you went to church! Listen, you little brat, you stay out of my sight, you. . . ."

"See you later."

"Far away, you traitor, this could cost me the presidency!"

Gently flowing in the stream of human compassion and humanitarian struggles for Utopia, a product of the "Get-To-Know-Your-Child" group might have the following meaningful relationship with her son:

"Mom, I can't make it for dinner tonight."

"I understand."

"I'm going to church."

"I understand."

"I believe in Jesus Christ as the Jewish Messiah."

"I understand."

"I'm a completed Jew!"

"I understand."

"Is that all you have to say?"

"No. Take out the trash before your father comes home."

Then, trapped in the "Think Young-Be Young" syndrome, a "teenage" matron might play the game this way:

"Mom, scratch me off the list for dinner tonight."

"Why, baby?"

"I'm going to eat dinner at church with some friends."

"That's cool."

"I believe in . . . Jesus."

"Funny you should say that, baby, 'cause your father and I were thinking about shaving our heads and chanting. Is there any difference?"

"Yes, mom. The difference between life and death."

"That's cool. Do your thing, man, but remember something."

"What's that?"

"I've got a splitting headache, so if this Jesus wants to crash here tonight the answer is 'no.' "[1]

---

1. Bob Friedman, *What's a Nice Jewish Boy Like You Doing in the First Baptist Church?* (Glendale, California: G/L Publications, 1972), pp. 15–20.

Now test your comprehension of "My Son, the Gentile" by answering the following questions:

.1. When a Jew discovers his Messiah his relatives will
- a. symbolically bury him in the family plot
- b. exile him to an Israeli kibbutz
- c. force him to see the rabbi
- d. all of the above

2. The most difficult person to persuade that your sanity is intact is
- a. father
- b. grandmother
- c. mother
- d. the rabbi

3. What kind of food did the traditional mother send out for?
- a. lox and bagels
- b. pizza
- c. chicken
- d. hamburgers

4. Where were the jet-set parents going for dinner?
- a. Berlin
- b. London
- c. Rome
- d. Paris

5. The third mother was a member of
- a. Hadassah
- b. Eastern Star
- c. Daughters of the American Revolution
- d. Job's Daughters

6. What office did she hold
- a. president
- b. vice-president
- c. secretary
- d. social chairman

7. Where was the son going for dinner in each case?
    a. the Hollywood Bowl
    b. church
    c. to the home of a friend
    d. out for a hamburger
8. The "Get-To-Know-Your-Child" mother reacted to her son's announcement by saying
    a. "Rabbi Gluckman should hear you now"
    b. "I understand"
    c. "Don't breathe a word of this to your father"
    d. "Stay out of my sight"
9. The reaction of the "Teenage" matron was
    a. indifference
    b. do your own thing
    c. forget it
    d. don't bug me
10. By what name or names did the son refer to his new belief?
    a. Christian
    b. Jewish-Christian
    c. completed Jew
    d. gentile Christian

Check your answers with those following. Give yourself ten points for each correct answer. Record on your Progress Chart the total number of points that you get correct. Do the same for the rest of the reading selections in this book.

1. d   3. c   5. a   7. b   9. b
2. c   4. d   6. a   8. b   10. b and c

How did you do? How does your speed and comprehension, while using the Wiggle, compare to your reading while using the Basic Z? Be sure that you have entered your wpm rate and comprehension estimate on your record sheet.

Practice the Wiggle again by reading for three more minutes in your novel. Record your wpm rate and comprehension.

Is there a difference this time? Did your rate go up? With practice and with the ease you gain each time you use a new pacing pattern, your reading speed will have a tendency to go up. As you come to each new pacing pattern, practice it at least twice before moving on to the next pacing pattern.

CURVE

When you feel comfortable with the Wiggle, practice the **Curve** shown below. The Curve is similar to the Basic Z, but instead of the pacing finger moving directly along the lines of print in rather straight, rigid movements, the Curve is a relaxed, more flowing motion which rounds off the ends of the lines.

Remember, the eyes are not following the path of the Curve, which is often cutting down into other lines, but are **reading along the lines of print.** Often the movement of the Curve pattern is a couple of lines below where the eyes are reading, but that movement is still visible and enables the eyes to keep moving and avoid regressions and unnecessarily long fixations.

One more point to remember as you practice this new movement: relax. Only if you are relaxed as you read will you be able to get a true feeling about the effectiveness of each motion.

Always enter your speed and comprehension for these readings on your record sheet.

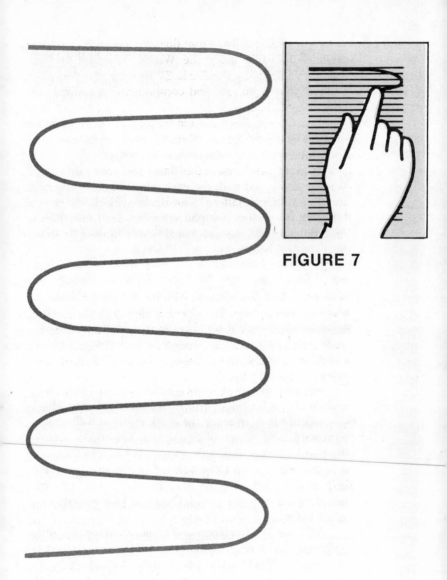

FIGURE 7

Now read the next selection included in this book while practicing the Curve. Calculate your wpm rate and define your comprehension on your record after you have also answered the questions following the reading.

"Tragedy at Sea"
An actual firsthand experience as relayed

by Tom Watson, Jr.

Shirley's watch stopped at exactly 10:20 A.M. on Saturday, July 24. At that moment our small boat capsized, throwing all of us into the sea and sealing the fate of our daughter Karen and our son Greg.

It seemed quite logical and safe when we nosed our 26-foot launch into the Pacific from the Koperapoka River on the south coast of West Irian (New Guinea). The ocean was smooth, and it was only a few miles to the mouth of the Tipoka. The shortcut across shallow tidal flats would save us several hours of travel along the winding rivers. We hoped to arrive in Kokonoa by early afternoon.

Because the resident missionaries at that coastal town were on furlough, The Evangelical Alliance Mission asked me to oversee the work there as well as in our own inland village of Sumapero. The trip between the two locations took only 45 minutes in a Missionary Aviation Fellowship Cessna, but a recent crash and the serious illness of an MAF pilot meant we must rely on the plywood launch John McCain had built several years before.

With its $3^{1}/_{2}$ horsepower Japanese engine, the little boat managed a respectable seven miles an hour—as long as the diesel fuel was reasonably free of water and the single-cylinder Yanma engine continued to fire.

We left Sumapero Thursday night, thinking how much Keith and Kathy, our two teenage children attending a mission school in the Philippines, would enjoy making the trip with us. Still, most of the cabin space was taken by Shirley and the three younger children. Moses Kujera, our national Christian friend, gave us navigation advice as I steered from a place on the foredeck.

By Friday night we had managed to cover about 74 miles on the Akimuga, Otakwa and Koperapoka Rivers. Dropping anchor, Moses speared small fish for bait, and Chipper, our 11-year-old, caught half a dozen catfish. These added welcome variety to the canned foods we had brought along.

—

Having no life preservers, and considering the boat unseaworthy in heavy weather, we had intended to make the entire trip via the winding rivers that form a network through the lowland swamp jungle of West Irian. But our fuel was running low, and a crocodile hunter told us he often paddled his dugout canoe across the calm ocean water between the mouths of the two rivers. With his reassurance—and with time and the prospect of a fuel shortage pressing us—we decided to take the shorter ocean route between the mouths of the Koperapoka and the Tipoka Rivers.

At seven o'clock Saturday morning we chugged from the Koperapoka channel southward into the Pacific. The tide was low, and we had to go ten miles from shore before turning west across the flats toward the mouth of the Tipoka. As we changed directions we noticed rain clouds were forming to the east and north, behind us. "Nothing to worry about," I said to Shirley. "Rain calms the sea."

But behind the rain shower a tremendous east wind arose, and by the time we decided the risk was growing too great it was impossible to reverse our course. Huge waves ran parallel to the shore, driving us along with them and threatening to swamp us each time we fell into a trough. Soon the coast line was obliterated by the storm. We felt as if we were a thousand miles from shore!

Chipper huddled in the little cabin with Karen and Gregory, our 2- and 4-year-olds. Shirley and Moses manned the bailing buckets while I tried to keep the boat headed in the direction the sea was running. We knew that letting it turn sideways would be disastrous.

The wave that stopped Shirley's watch was nearly 20 feet high—a roaring monster that came in from one side and rolled the boat completely over like a toy in a bathtub. Moses and I were thrown into the sea and had to swim for our lives back to the overturned launch. Chipper managed to escape from the flooded cabin, while Shirley retrieved the two younger children through the sliding door. Only then did we realize how truly grave our situation was. Until the boat capsized, we were frightened but confident. Now, clinging to the slippery sides and pounded by a succession of murderous waves, we were forced to face the fact that some of us might not survive this terrible experience.

—

Chipper became our first hero. When the anchor we were dragging dug into a sandbar and sent the boat into wild gyrations, it was our brave boy who saved us. He managed to break the anchor's grip on the bottom and secure it to the upturned bow of the boat. Once again we were floating free.

"It's fun swimming in the water, Daddy," Greg

said to me as I held him with one arm, "but I want to go home and get a drink of milk." A few moments later a wave larger than the rest swept him from my weakened grasp and left him face down in the sea some 50 feet away. By the time I got him and then struggled back to the overturned boat, our next-to-youngest was gone. We were too dazed and exhausted to weep.

Moses made a superhuman effort to save Karen's life. At grave risk to himself he held our baby in one arm and clung desperately to the boat's hull with the other. But when we struck another sandbar at about 3 P.M. and our boat began breaking up—still some five miles from shore—we felt the end had come. One of the incredibly powerful waves snatched Karen from Moses' grip, and it seemed futile to hold Greg's body any longer. Now both of our little ones were with the Lord.

Shirley was at the end of her endurance, and the loss of our children had robbed her of the will to struggle against the elements any longer. But a sheet of plywood, which the waves had torn from the boat's canopy, proved sufficient to support her weight, and I felt if God would give me strength I might be able to push her to an island lying a few miles to the northwest.

Chipper and Moses took small pieces of wreckage from the boat and decided to strike out on their own. It seemed worth the risk. In fact, as we watched them struggle slowly toward the distant shore in the teeth of an outgoing tide, I felt their chances were considerably better than our own.

Shirley and I made good progress, and for a while it seemed that with a bit of cooperation from wind and current we would make it to the beach. But the closer we got to the island, the stronger the current became on a course at right angles to our goal. We got within a hundred yards of the shore before it became impossible to narrow the distance any further.

—

Simultaneously, as hope diminished to nothing, our thoughts went to Keith and Kathy in Manila. Greg and Karen were gone. Chipper very likely had failed to make it to shore. What would it be like for our two oldest suddenly to learn they were the "only survivors?" What would be the reactions of Christians in the homeland to the fact that God had allowed a thing like this to happen to missionaries they were supporting? Or that people in God's service had allowed themselves to get into such a hazardous situation?

It was at that moment of despair that Shirley spoke quietly of a gospel song she had sung as a member of the freshman choir back at Columbia (S.C.) Bible College: "The mighty billows are high, but the Lord is above them and mighty."

Could we believe that the promises of His presence, His awareness, and His love apply even in circumstances such as these?

"All things work together for good to them that love God." I repeated the familiar words from Romans 8:28, and together we began to see the Word of God in a new light. Not a rabbit's foot to stroke against the threat of bad luck. Not a fetish to ward off pain, loss or unpleasant circumstances. But a dependable contract guaranteeing that the goodness and the love of God override every situation to provide what will ultimately be seen as life's very best!

With hearts bowed before His sovereignty, we suddenly felt our feet touch bottom in the trough of one of the waves. We were crossing a sand bar extending from a small peninsula on the island! A few moments later our plywood raft caught on the stump of a dead tree. At 7 P.M., by my waterproof watch, we staggered ashore as darkness fell, too weary even to stand.

A light rain was still falling, and both of us were suffering from the cold. When we regained our strength we decided it would be best to build a small lean-to and try to sleep until morning. It was soon apparent though that the gnats and mosquitos would make that impossible. Since the tide would soon be out, we felt it would be well to see how deep the channel between the island and the mainland would be when the tide was lowest. We could not have timed it better! In the darkness we could see only a few feet ahead, but as we inched forward we found only mud. We had to move on our hands and knees, but we covered every foot with praise and thanksgiving. By midnight we were safe at last on the south coast of West Irian.

—

Do I dare say "safe"? We still had only a vague idea of our position. We had serious doubts about Chipper's and Moses' safety. We had neither water nor food. But we figured that with good fortune we might be no more than ten or twelve miles from an Indonesian sulphur mine at the village of Amamperay. It seemed a good idea to continue moving in that direction.

Our bare feet were no match for the clam shells, vines and sharp roots, but we had no choice but a route through the jungle just above the shore line. The incoming tide made it impossible to walk on the beach.

As the sun rose through breaking storm clouds, we

reached the mouth of the Tipoka River and knew that we were not far from the mining camp. There were two small tributaries to be crossed, but we felt, after all we had been through, that God surely would provide a way across these rivers.

And we were right. When we reached the first tributary we stumbled upon some islander's abandoned bivouac and found the bottom of an old dugout canoe. Shirley sat on the shore while I paddled across the open water on my makeshift surfboard. Some 30 minutes later I reached the second small river and stood at last in full view of the mining camp upriver across the wide Tipoka.

But though I could see native workers in the distance, they could not hear my shouts. I had reason to doubt that I had strength to swim across the Tipoka, but to be so close and give up seemed out of the question. With a prayer for enablement on my lips, I floated on my back and began to kick and paddle toward the other shore.

My watch showed 10 A.M. when some of the Mimika laborers saw me struggling through the last 200 yards of mud between the river and the camp. It is hard to imagine how I must have appeared to them—a bedraggled white man slogging toward the camp out of the river's slime!

They were kind. Tenderly they carried me to the camp, where they dressed my cuts and offered me a glass of warm milk.

By the time the mining company's boat reached Shirley, Chipper and Moses had already joined her. We had reached the same island, but Chipper and Moses had slept from sheer exhaustion. In the morning they had discovered our tracks and had followed them eastward to the Tipoka and northward to the first tributary where Shirley was waiting. Within minutes after we were all reunited, the mining company's helicopter had come to take us 40 miles inland to a small hospital. Two days later we were picked up by an MAF Cessna and flown to the mission base at Sentani.

There it became my duty to file our "accident report". Accident? In terms of human understanding it was surely that—an accident so tragic that its memory will overwhelm us for years to come. It is not difficult in retrospect to think of common sense ways the terrible loss could have been avoided.

Yet somehow overriding the errors and frailty of our own humanity there lies the grace and goodness of Jesus Christ, whose servants we are. Shirley and I are convinced that all things in due time become benefit, when committed to His good hands.[2]

2. Larry Rascher, "Tragedy at Sea," *Today,* October 1, 1972, (Evanston, Illinois: Harvest Publications, 1972).

Now test your comprehension of "Tragedy at Sea" by answering the following questions:

1. At the time of the accident the Watsons were traveling in a
   - a. dugout canoe
   - b. sailboat
   - c. raft
   - d. plywood launch
2. The missionaries were stationed in
   - a. the Philippines
   - b. Sumatra
   - c. West Irian
   - d. the New Hebrides
3. They were overseeing the work in the coastal village because
   - a. there were no missionaries to place there
   - b. the resident missionaries were ill
   - c. the resident missionaries were on furlough
   - d. the resident missionaries were killed in a plane crash
4. It was necessary to make the trip by boat rather than plane because
   - a. of a recent crash
   - b. there was no place to land a plane
   - c. the pilot was seriously ill
   - d. both a and c
   - e. both b and c
5. The wave that overturned the boat was
   - a. 7 feet high
   - b. 10 feet high
   - c. 20 feet high
   - d. 30 feet high

6. Chipper proved to be a hero by
 a. catching catfish for dinner
 b. manning the bailing buckets
 c. breaking the anchor's grip on the bottom and securing it to the upturned bow
 d. holding Karen while clinging desperately to the hull
7. The two oldest children were
 a. lost at sea
 b. away at school
 c. left behind at their own station
8. After reaching the island it was impossible for them to get any sleep because of the
 a. falling rain
 b. high tide
 c. strong wind
 d. gnats and mosquitoes
9. They finally reached help at a(n)
 a. native village
 b. Indonesian sulphur mine
 c. diamond mine
 d. mission station
10. They were taken inland to a small hospital by
 a. MAF Cessna
 b. helicopter
 c. boat across the Tipoka

You can check your answers with those following. As before, give yourself ten points for each correct answer and record the results on your Progress Chart.

1. d 3. c 5. c 7. b 9. b
2. c 4. d 6. c 8. d 10. b

How did you do this time?

While using your novel or any other reading material, continue practicing the Curve until you feel comfortable using it. Practice this pacing movement in a five-minute drill. Calculate your wpm rate and define your comprehension on your record sheet.

LOOP

Another pacing movement is the **Loop,** which will rapidly increase your speed. First look at the illustration of the Loop (see Figure 8) and then read the description of its application.

As with the Basic Z and Curve, this movement is done with the index finger and is a relaxed gliding of the finger across the line and then, instead of curving down at the end of the line, looping up and back to the beginning of the second line where a second upward loop is made to reverse direction and start reading across the next line. Caution: the loops at the beginning and ending of each line should be very small. In fact, for those who prefer the Loop, there is a tendency to develop something of a swinging, back-and-forth effect in pacing. Before you try this on your reading selection you may want to trace over the Loop pattern several times. (See Figure 8.)

Be certain that you have recorded your reading score from the last reading selection. Then practice the Loop pacing movement in the following reading exercise. And after that, answer the comprehension questions following the selection. Again, record your results.

"Where Are Those Resignation Forms?"

Thank you, boys and girls, for that good singing. My, that was nice. I bet they heard us all the way down to the United. . . . Yes, Gary? Oh, they *did* complain? Well, next time we'll shut the windows when we use that song.

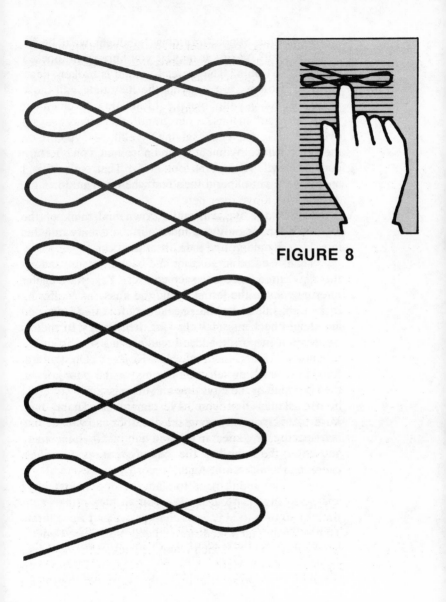

FIGURE 8

Now, this Sunday morning I thought we'd begin.
. . . Yes, Gail? Yes, you may, if you hurry right back. I
thought . . . Robin? The water fountain is broken, dear.
All right. Now we are studying the Beatitudes, all those
verses beginning with "blessed." John, do you remember
what "blessed" means? Your grandfather always says it
over the turkey at Thanksgiving? Wellll, yes, you are on
the right track. Arthur? Maureen spit at you? Return
good for evil, Arthur. No, no, NO! That isn't what I
meant. Now get paper towels and when you are through,
Arthur may move over here.

Now class, we will settle down and think of the
lesson. We have only one-half hour . . . twenty minutes
left. Jane, would you see who's at the door?

Thank you, Miss Koffner. Yes, I will be sure and get
the new attendance records correct. Yes, the regular
offering goes in the left side and the missionary offering
in the right side and a blue check mark for attendance and
an orange check mark for carrying their Bibles. Birthdays
get written in purple and a handkerchief sent from the
Sunday School. Thank you, Miss Koff. . . . Oh, the first
Sunday of each month the offering for the *poor* goes in
the right side of the envelope and the missionary offering
in a basket? Of course, I'll remember. Thank you,
Miss. . . . Harry Keen is outside the door and won't come
in? Because he's late? Well, send him in. Oh, latecomers
get sent to the main desk for a green excuse and I make a
check mark in the. . . .

Well, she didn't need to slam the door! Now, boys
and girls, the Beatitudes. Will you all please take your
Bibles and turn to Matthew, chapter five and verse three.
That's the hymnbook, Karen, the Bible has red edges.
Look, about one-half inch from the back of the book. All
right? Book of Matthew. Robin, what *is* it? No, you
certainly can't go next door to the parsonage and get a

drink. You must take your allergy pill? Do you have a written note from your mother? I am not supposed to approve pills. . . . No, no, do *not* go out in the choir and ask her. Let me think a minute. You are *positive* it's an allergy pill? Alvin, that is enough! Allergy pills are *not* the same as dope. Dear me, Robin, I hardly. . . . All right, go next door and get a drink. What? Well, if you can swallow it without water, why did. . .?

Class! Please quiet down now and think. "Blessed are the poor in spirit, for theirs is the kingdom of heaven." Now I really want you to *think* of what that means. Cora, see who's knocking, please. Yes, Mr. Snerb, I know the teacher's meeting is Monday at seven. I will be there provided I have the car. Serve on the Jello and Cucumber Salad Committee for the picnic? Wellll, can I let you know?

Now, children, the "poor in spirit." Just a minute, Bea, we will *not* name names of those who may be poor in material things. No, the Huggins are *not* the worst family in the. . . . Now, stop right there. You are missing the point "Poor in spirit." What is "spirit"? Shhh, they can hear you laughing in the sanctuary! I did *not* say spirits, I said. . . . Yes, Barbara. Like a ghost? Well, that shows you're thinking.

Sam? You don't understand why the poor should be happy? Yes, I know that "blessed" means happy and favored. And I know your father can read Greek. He said to tell me? Sam, I have an English-Greek concordance of my own, and I check many of the words from the text. Don't know nothin' from beans? Whatever could he have meant by *that?* I realize this is only my second year of teaching. . . . Never mind, Sam, thank you for helping. And I will try to answer your question. Why did Jesus say the poor were happy? It does sound strange, doesn't it? I'm not quite sure. . . .

Margie, you wanted to know what the "kingdom" is? Why, I think it is safe to say it is whatever the King will give. Yes, I don't think anyone would argue with that. If I said a real kingdom, you would ask me to see it. And if I said an invisible kingdom. . . . No, I am *not* mixed up, Billy. It's just that we have ten minutes left and it's hot in here and I am supposed to give you a written test and we're still on the first verse!

Now, on to the next verse. "They that mourn." Mourn is used in the sense of being sorry, and those who are sorry for doing wrong will someday be happy they mourned. . . . Oh, good morning, Mrs. Castner. You would like to visit our class? Do come in, we are just finishing. The clocks are wrong and I have another quarter hour? Good. Harry, bring Mrs. Castner a chair. *One* chair, I said. I do not think you are at all funny.

Now, the "meek." What is "meek"? Kenneth? I *know* it rhymes with "squeak," I didn't ask you. . . . Class! That is enough! "Meek" rhymes with many things, but the point is, what does it mean? Mush-mouthed? Oh, I hardly. . . . Beaten down? Stupid? No, no, I think we are getting away from the original meaning of being patient under suffering.

Raise your hand, Charles, don't just call out. Your last teacher was too meek and that's why she quit? And you helped her by finding the resignation forms in the back of the cupboard? I really didn't know Miss Nadette very well. No, she did *not* have a nervous breakdown, she moved to Florida! You are being rude.

Jan, please read the next verse. Hunger and thirst after *what?* Go on. You're so hungry your stomach is making weird noises? Well, it *is* five minutes after twelve, but be patient, the reverend is going a bit overtime. However, we are speaking of. . . . Joseph Bender, we do *not* repeat remarks we may have heard about the minister. I don't care if your father *did* say so!

All right class. . . . Donna, if you are sick, dear, go and lie down in the restroom. The Boy Scouts borrowed the cot for the weekend? Oh, dear, are you really ill? Lean your head against the piano, dear, until I find. . . . Oh, dear. What *is* it, Arthur, must you bother me now? You're sick, too? And Robin? Sam? Why, I thought the epidemic of stomach virus was over, you can't *all* be getting sick. And so suddenly. I think you are just doing this to. . . .

Charles, look in the back of the cupboard and see if there isn't one of those resignation forms left! Hurry!

EPILOGUE

Of course I didn't really resign. I made sure I got lots of sleep that week to recuperate, then I took a good, long look at what I could do to keep other Sunday mornings from being like the imaginary one described here.

To begin with, I laid down the rule that no one leaves during the hour. Personal needs must be attended to before or after class. Then I recruited one of the girls as secretary to take the attendance during the singing. We settled the offering interruption by placing the basket by the door where children could leave their gifts as they entered.

At the teacher's meeting that week, I brought up the problem of other interruptions. It was agreed that a teacher is not to be interrupted by *anyone*—not *anyone!*

My lesson presentation was *not* holding them spellbound, that was obvious! So I determined to spend more time studying and to bring some pertinent objects or visual aids with me. An interesting lesson would eliminate much of the chatter and irrelevant remarks. Discussion questions help meet their need to talk and meet the learning aim, too! Including other Bible learning activities to involve the students, such as interviewing a "Bible character" or writing a poem or short story about a Bible truth, helps the students reach the learning aim.

And to think I could get so busy all week that I did not know I was using last year's lessons! I resolved to stay home several nights a week in place of the activities and volunteer work I was doing.

And early to bed Saturday night would find me refreshed and relaxed Sunday morning, not likely to get so flustered or annoyed over incidents.

Each pupil should have his own Bible and get to know it well. I have a feeling the Sunday School would be willing to purchase them for pupils who have none in the home.

I resolved not only to be a teacher, but to be a *good* teacher! I signed up to attend an out-of-town convention for teachers and workers, and joined a teacher training class.

Since I am new at teaching, I asked a teacher of some twenty years' experience, who is not teaching now, to sit in on my classes and give me helpful criticism afterward. She will help me spot the defects—like forgetting to open with prayer, not knowing how to help my students *apply* the lesson to their lives—and she will suggest how I can improve my teaching ministry.

I am spending more time with my students. I occasionally visit them in their homes and chat with them on the telephone. I'm getting to know them and their needs. Learning more about my students helps them learn more Sunday morning.[3]

3. Lois Hoadley Dick, "Where Are Those Resignation Forms?" *Teach* magazine, Spring Quarter 1973 (Glendale, California: G/L Publications, 1972).

Now test your comprehension of "Where Are Those Resignation Forms?" by answering the following questions:

1. The class was studying
   - a. The Lord's Prayer
   - b. The feeding of the five thousand
   - c. The Beatitudes
   - d. The Golden Rule
2. Robin's problem involved
   - a. taking an allergy pill
   - b. a bad cold
   - c. an itchy rash
   - d. inability to sit still
3. Mr. Snerb stopped by to
   - a. ask them to be quieter
   - b. request her to be on the Jello and Cucumber Salad Committee
   - c. observe her new teaching techniques
   - d. bring the Sunday School papers
4. Sam's father
   - a. thought she was a good teacher
   - b. never discussed anything with Sam
   - c. could read Greek
   - d. was a seminary professor
5. Attendance records were
   - a. very easy to use
   - b. unnecessarily complicated
   - c. unorganized and poorly administered
   - d. not kept
6. The teacher
   - a. resigned
   - b. became ill the next Sunday
   - c. resolved to be a good teacher
   - d. moved to Florida to be with Miss Nadette

7. New classroom rules for the students included
   a. attending to personal needs before class
   b. no whispering
   c. separation of boys and girls
   d. all of the above
8. The teacher's steps to do a better job included
   a. resignation from the local women's club
   b. more time in personal devotions
   c. joining a teacher training class
   d. reading the Bible every day
9. The observer she invited to evaluate her teaching was
   a. a public school teacher
   b. a favorite Bible teacher
   c. the Sunday School superintendent
   d. a teacher with twenty years' experience
10. Personal contact with her students
    a. helps to maintain discipline
    b. creates a warm relationship with their parents
    c. helps them to learn more on Sunday morning
    d. keeps them interested in the class

| 1. c | 3. b | 5. b | 7. a | 9. d |
| 2. a | 4. c | 6. c | 8. c | 10. c |

The Loop has become a favorite pacing motion because it is relaxing and still allows for a high speed in reading. Practice the Loop pacing movement in your novel for several minutes. Then check to see how rapidly you can read using the Loop in a five-minute drill in your novel. Record your score and comprehension and compare it with your other reading rates.

By the way, don't be discouraged if your progress chart seems to be fluctuating—that's normal. Depending on things like interest, familiarity, your degree of fatigue, your score will go up and down. What is important to watch is the **trend** of your scores. That should be going up.

Begin reading. . . .

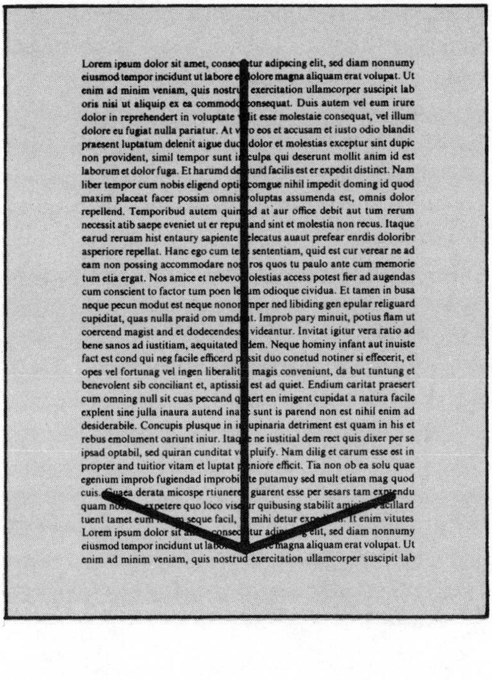

FIGURE 9

ARROW

After you have recorded your score for the Loop, try the **Arrow** pacing motion as shown in Figure 9.

In moving the finger straight down the page your eyes are still reading across the line, but are being pulled from line to line at a steady pace. The Arrow can be practiced with one or two fingers, down the center or margins of the page. Or instead of your fingers, you can use a card, ruler, or straight edge. If you use a card, try slanting the left corner of the card at an angle that exposes the beginning of each new line. As you pull the

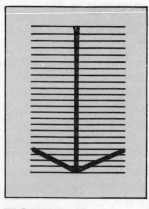

FIGURE 10

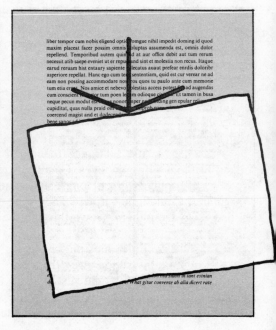

card down, the tilted card acts as a very effective pacer, in effect pulling your eyes across the line as well as down the page. This pacing movement is for the individual who feels uncomfortable with a lot of movement on the page as he reads, or for the person who feels that his eyes want to work ahead of his hand.

Practice the Arrow pacing motion and its variations while reading the next selection. Remember to time yourself. Begin immediately.

"A Merry Heart"

It happened one Sunday afternoon when the boys and I were having dinner at a mountain lodge. We were just beginning our soup when I was called to the phone. Both boys scraped their chairs back and leapt to their feet when I arose, a display of gallantry that gave me a bit of a jolt and prompted me to go whole hog and say, "Will you excuse me, please?"

When I went back to the table, they were engrossed in conversation, but when they saw me coming they leapt up again, and with more scraping of chairs, got me and themselves seated.

This all gave me a strange feeling of unreality. I looked at them with new eyes. Could this mean that all my years of training were, at long last, bearing fruit? Was I dreaming? Could it be—it *was!* They were dipping their spoons *away* from them! Down through the years I had said:

> "Like little ships put out to sea
> I dip my spoon away from me"

without success. They would just join in and repeat it mechanically along with me. They knew the poem but the connection between the poem and its application escaped them somehow. And now, here they were, dipping away, as if they'd been doing it all their lives.

As if this were not enough of a shock, the conversation took several interesting twists and I realized they were cognizant of what was going on in the world, had some serious views of life—and in passing—noticed that they were even pronouncing their participles. I looked at them with their clean necks, their hair plastered down with alarming neatness, their fine manners, and felt like somebody else. And, like Jane in the story, the years turned back. Not categorically, of course. The events that flashed through my mind were haphazard and unrelated.

My first ideals and ideas about parenthood, for instance. I tackled motherhood with a fanatic thoroughness that appalled my friends, alarmed my poor mother, and all but finished us off. My sterile efficiency was enough to make any discriminating baby roll up his personal accouterments in a diaper and leave home. Surely the uncertain fortunes of the world could not be worse than the certain misfortune of being in the hands of this grim woman.

As I see it now, the basic problem was my absolute lack of flexibility. At this age of development, if we were on page 36, we had better *be* on page 36. If they were on page 35 or 37, it was a horrible reflection on my ability as a mother and could not be tolerated. And so we lived by pages and chapters. We lived by the thermometer, too, until the day I phoned our doctor for the drillionth time and reported a temperature of 101. I asked him what I should do and he said wearily, "Break the thermometer."

Fun moments? Of course. Sawhorses hitched to the back porch, to be leapt on at a moment's notice, to gallop over the plains and carry a secret message to the king. Or to gallop to a secret hide-out (converted piano box at the end of the yard) to eat lunch. And sometimes lunch eaten while the three of us solemnly wore paper rabbit ears and called each other Flopsie, Mopsie and Mother Cottontail—so the dreadful carrots would taste better. And stories. Millions of them. All the Bible stories. And a continued story concerning the adventures of a certain Gary Wayne Sinkstopper and Stephen Paul Wastebasket, which literally ran for years.

But it is not the successful times I want to talk about, for we do not learn from success—and we do not identify ourselves with, or expect any understanding or help from a paragon of success. Success *inspires,* to be sure. But it's from our failures—and other people's failures—that we learn.

But back to the mountain lodge and the story. Other memories in the flash back that day crept into the story. Gary's sliding down the bannister and landing with a resounding thud on the back of an unsuspecting guest who was standing in the hallway. The dismal failure of attempted piano lessons. Report cards.

Oh. And the day we were swimming at a conference in the east. We went through the you - can't - do - that - but - the - other - kids - are - doing - it - but - you're - a - speaker's - kid - you - can't - behave - like - those - other - kids routine. So Gary did it. He went down the water slide head first and plunged head down through the water, sinking himself like a fence post into the lake bottom.

They laid him on the beach, and a preliminary examination by the camp doctor disclosed a possible fractured vertebra. Gary cut his teeth on medical terminology and was not fooled for an instant. "I've got a broken neck," he shrieked. Now a broken neck for some reason sounds more ominous than a fractured vertebra. It suggests the head hanging off to one side.

So it was a solemn and sober little party that entered

the ambulance for the fifty-mile ride to the nearest hospital. The ride, it turned out, was fun in a weird sort of way. To see the cars ducking and scurrying off to both sides of the road in response to the ambulance siren gave an odd sense of power and exhilaration. I had trouble with my driving for weeks afterward. I still thought I had the undisputed right of way.

As Gary could not raise his head, I gave him my vanity case mirror so he could see the fun. He was beginning to enjoy the whole thing.

The attention lavished on him at the hospital was something to behold. Gary was almost disappointed to find his neck wasn't broken after all. There was nothing wrong that five days of traction didn't fix up.

And then there was Steve's broken leg. Done in a most undramatic way. A falling truck tailgate. Humiliating. If a boy is going to crack a bone, he wants a tale of derring-do connected with it—something you can get your teeth into.

A cast was put on the leg and a week later I went off on tour leaving the boys safely boarded in the mountains. Steve's cast was no drawback at all. He had circumvented all obstacles and could do just about anything. For the first week I was only a few hundred miles up the coast and we exchanged letters. But before I took off for New York I thought a phone call was in order. I talked to them both at once.

"How are you?" I said.

"I'm okay," said Steve.

"He's okay," said Gary.

"How's everything at camp?" I offered. "D'you think it's safe for me to go east?"

"That's okay," said Steve.

"That's okay," said Gary.

"Are you *sure* you're all right?" I persisted.

"I'm okay," said Steve.

"He's okay," said Gary.

"Well, all right then. Goodbye," I said.

"Goodbye, mother. Oh. Except that I shot myself," said Steve.

"Yeah, tell her about shooting yourself," said Gary.

"It was an accident," said Steve. "And it's only a flesh wound. I had a tetanus shot at the hospital. It's okay."

"And the rattlesnake bite." Gary was beginning to recover his memory.

"It's okay," said Steve. "I had an anti-snake shot at the hospital."

The silence that followed was punctuated by my heavy breathing.

"Why didn't you tell me?" I said in low-pressured tones—an effort to control myself. "We've been talking for five minutes. Why didn't you tell me? I *asked* you a dozen times how you were."

"It all happened in the *other* leg," said Steve. "You didn't *ask* about that one."

—

But back again to the mountain lodge. We finished dinner, they calculated the tip, paid the bill, helped me into my wrap, helped me into the car, all with impeccable finesse, and we went on our way. I looked at Steve. "You're okay," I thought. And at Gary. "You're okay," I thought. And at our life together. "It's okay," I thought.

We bring our children up with deadly seriousness, with a welter of charts and graphs, comparing them with the "norm" and looking at them with a jaundiced eye if they do not hit it. We lose sight of the fact that there *is* no norm.

Don't compare your child with other children—or with page 36. Look at them and it, if you will, but don't compare. Your child is *your* child—not somebody else's child or the child on page 36. He is the sum total of his genes and chromosomes and his environment. He is *him.* Accept him as he is, God bless him, and don't try to make him someone else. Is he slow to learn? Edison was sent home from school because he apparently could not learn anything. Abe Lincoln's whole life was a pattern of apparent failure until he became President.

On the human side, a sense of humor is one of the best traits you can have for parenthood. It smooths out the rocky places. The serious should not be discounted of course. The Bible teaches:

Train up a child in the way he should go: and when he is old, he will not depart from it (Proverbs 22:6).

He that spareth his rod hateth his son: but he that loveth him chasteneth him betimes (Proverbs 13:24).

And these words, which I command thee this day, shall be in thine heart: And thou shalt teach them diligently unto thy children . . . (Deuteronomy 6:6,7).

But the Scriptures also tell us:

A merry heart maketh a cheerful countenance . . . he that is of a merry heart hath a continual feast . . . a merry heart doeth good like medicine (Proverbs 15:13,15; 17:22).

And Jesus said:

These things have I spoken unto you, that my joy might remain in you, and that your joy might be full (John 15:11).

Christ Himself enjoyed sociability and fellowship. I am inclined to think He enjoyed merriment, too, at the proper times and places. And I suppose that is, after all, the crux of the whole problem. In Ecclesiastes 3:1,4 we are told: "To every thing there is a season, and a time to every purpose under the heaven: . . . A time to weep, and a time to laugh. . . ."

If we can discern the proper times for seriousness and the proper time for love and laughter—and get the correct ratio—we have, with prayer, an unbeatable formula from the Word of God. And The Word of God gives us the blessed therapeutic heart-warming privilege of merriment to relieve the tension, add spice to the humdrum and alleviate the deadly serious business of being a parent.

Laughs? We had a million of them. But, looking back, I can see where we could have had a million more. Alas, we did not. And the fault is mine.[4]

4. Ethel Barrett, "A Merry Heart," *Teach* magazine, Winter Quarter 1965 (Glendale, California: G/L Publications, 1965).

Now test your comprehension of "A Merry Heart" by answering the following questions:

1. The author was having dinner
   a. at the home of friends
   b. at a mountain lodge
   c. at a hotel dining room
   d. at camp
2. She was surprised when she realized her sons
   a. were cognizant of what was going on in the world
   b. had some serious views of life
   c. were dipping their spoons away from them
   d. all of the above
3. The events that flashed through her mind were
   a. orderly and related
   b. haphazard and unrelated
   c. startling
4. One of her first basic problems of parenthood was her
   a. flexibility
   b. domineering ways
   c. disinterest
   d. absolute lack of flexibility
5. During a swimming accident Gary sustained a
   a. broken neck
   b. fractured vertebra
   c. broken leg
   d. none of the above
6. Steve suffered a broken leg
   a. while sliding down the bannister
   b. in a skiing accident
   c. from a falling truck tailgate
   d. by shooting himself

7. She left the boys at a camp
   a. in the woods
   b. by a lake
   c. in the mountains
   d. on a western ranch
8. Two famous men the author mentions are
   a. Washington and Lincoln
   b. Franklin and Adams
   c. Edison and Lincoln
   d. Roosevelt and Truman
9. From the human standpoint, one of the best traits you can have as a parent is
   a. a good sense of humor
   b. a good sense of discipline
   c. fairness
   d. an abundance of love
10. The author quotes verses on a merry heart from the book of
    a. Psalms
    b. Proverbs
    c. Ecclesiastes
    d. John

1. b	3. b	5. d	7. c	9. a
2. d	4. d	6. c	8. c	10. b

4

FOUR MORE ADVANCED PACING
TECHNIQUES

In the following section you will review four more pacing movements. Don't go any further, however, until you have spent time practicing the last four comfort patterns. As you practice each movement on your novel and any other practice reading, you may find a pacing motion especially suited to your needs.

The four new pacing movements are called **Crosshatch, Zig-Zag, Spiral** and **Hop.**

CROSSHATCH

The **Crosshatch** movement is a little bit different in that it may be done with two fingers. (See Figure 11.) Illustration 1 shows the general pattern. Illustration 2 shows how to run your index finger in a relaxed movement across the page. Illustration 3 shows the return sweep being made with the second finger.

This motion looks a lot more complicated than it really is. With a slight flicking of two fingers (one finger across, a second finger back) you will find a relaxing pacing motion that may be particularly helpful in increasing your reading efficiency. Remember, your eyes still read every word. It doesn't matter what pattern is used, it simply provides "pull" and rhythm for your eye movement.

After practicing the Crosshatch for a few minutes, or until you can pace fairly comfortably, read the next selection in this book.

Bob Friedman and Jesus

It is only after I became a believer in the Messiah that I began to reflect upon my past life in an attempt to

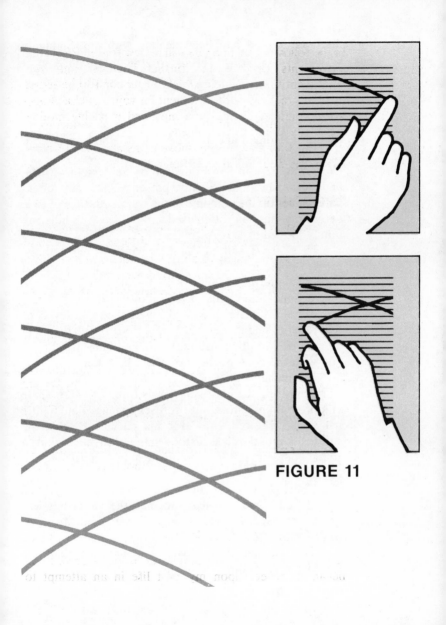

FIGURE 11

discover if God had been dealing with me. Suddenly certain events flashed through my memory banks and I imagined God's voice reverberating:

"Ah, ha! So you think I've left you alone, eh?"

Then I had to admit I had always been plagued with a nagging knowledge of this Jesus. A sort of seriocomedy of Bob Friedman and Jesus. Me first. Him—away back there in the shadows.

I was born in San Francisco on September 4, 1943, and seriously doubt if my presence had any effect whatsoever on the outcome of the war. At the age of two, before my legs had gotten used to the Bay City's hills, my family moved to Los Angeles.

In 1950 we shifted our belongings to my parents' present home in Santa Monica. A gentile neighborhood with a smattering of Jews. Like finding a few good rye breads amidst hundreds of loaves of white.

My oldest sister Judy and I were the real "Jews" of the family, taking our faith more seriously than my parents or two other sisters, Linda and Pam. But I'll hit you with the consequences of this a little later.

Meanwhile—at Roosevelt Grammar School. At Christmastime the entire class was forced to participate in a program of carols, but I refused to sing about a little baby who chewed straw for his pacifier. Being the shortest kid in the class, I stood in the front, not making a sound, but moving my mouth in hopes of fooling the teacher.

Come to think of it, maybe she wasn't fooled. At one time I had wanted to learn to play the violin but was quickly refused. I couldn't sing "Three Blind Mice" on key.

This was ridiculous. It was just a new key, that's all. Instead of rewarding me for my inventive talents in the world of music they simply concluded I was the most horrible singer in modern history.

Dozens of people have since confirmed this, but what does that prove? I still think it's a completely new key.

I had inherited my inventive abilities from my father. When he was fourteen he dreamed up the self-winding wrist watch, but didn't know what to do with it. Years later he sold the "clear" cartridge idea to Sheaffer's so users of fountain pens could determine how much ink remained.

Yet although he invented dozens of practical and commercial things he seemed satisfied to stay with his baby: a corrugated drinking tube, called the Flex-Straw, which became an instant success with hospitals as well as housewives.

When I was very young we did have a Christmas tree. As a thing of beauty. It smells good, right? Yet after I began attending Sunday School and learning a thing or two I refused to let that pagan symbol into our home.

Pam was heartbroken. She loved trees. Linda loved trees as long as they were still in the ground on a mountain slope, while my parents were apathetic. Judy was on my side and we won out. No tree.

Like good Jewish families everywhere we celebrated Chanukah and its feast of lights. I really enjoyed this and made sure the whispering and jokes had ceased before saying the Hebrew prayer over the candles.

Although I was very serious about it, the last two words of the prayer are ". . . shel Chanukah" and it was difficult for me not to think of a gas station.

At Sunday School we'd goof off with the other kids and avoid the rabbi. We assumed he had a horrible sense of humor. The Bible stories were only that—stories.

Once in a while our teacher would interject a scientific explanation for a biblical miracle.

Never, never, in this reform temple did anyone mention a *personal* God. A God who cared about us, loved us, took care of us and knew when we passed notes behind the teacher's back.

My parents went to temple very seldom. My father was raised in an Orthodox home and he had received his quota of religion at an early age. God was not a subject we discussed at home, due to indifference rather than hostility.

Yet each year we held a Passover seder for the family. Lamb shank. Hard-boiled egg. Parsley. The whole works. Dad would tediously go through the Haggadah, the book outlining the service, although in later years not enough members of our group had the patience for a seder so it was given up.

How could I blame them? It did seem a bit foolish to force yourself to go through a ritual because it was expected of you. One year Pam had almost put the finishing blow on the entire scene.

It's customary to "open the door" for Elijah, the great Jewish prophet who someday would announce the coming of the Messiah. For many Orthodox Jews this is a very real hope.

We hadn't noticed Pam was missing from the table. Then, when the door for Elijah was opened, she came walking in with a towel draped over her head and her teeth clamped tight to muffle the giggles.

I was furious! This was a crushing blow to my efforts to have a respectable seder.

After being graduated from high school I served in the army reserve for six months' active duty at Ft. Ord, California, near Monterey.

Wow, man. Here come the Southerners. My first exposure to these folks I had just seen in movies.

"Hey, man, how do ya spell stamp?" one asked me.

"Stamp?"

"Yeah, uh, huh."

"S - T - A - M - P - Q."

"P - Q?"

"Yeah, uh, huh."

"Thanks, man."

Of course these dudes weren't the cream of the Dixie brain trust, but as far as I knew they were. Immediately I saw one wearing a cross and concluded it was necessary to commit intellectual suicide to become a Christian.

All the other gentiles, or Christians as I thought, who had a little something going for them upstairs yet still went to church must have ulterior motives. To recruit for the Elks Club, maybe.

It was a definite advantage to have "Jewish" stamped on your dog tags since this meant we received three three-day passes during the High Holy Days. A Catholic friend was infuriated when I told him I was going to get another pass for Cha-*noo*-kah.

If I had pronounced Chanukah correctly it would have lost something of its humorous impact.

After a year and a half at San Diego State, during which time I made horrible grades, I decided to take a break and work in San Francisco for a while.

My educational achievements were always disappointing. I rebelled against my parents' pushing me to get good marks, so considered it a real challenge to see how well I could do on tests with no study time under my belt.

In high school I had made straight A's in math and had done well in science and English classes—due strictly to my ability to pick things up quickly in class (not because I actually sat down on my *own* time and studied!).

San Diego State had wanted me to take all those advanced courses for the "elite" after I finished in the top two percent of their entrance examination, but I declined. Work harder? Forget it.

I stumbled from semester to semester with no real purpose other than that of obtaining a piece of paper my father could hang on his wall under those of my three sisters. They had all been graduated from U.C.L.A.

In San Francisco I got a "job" selling encyclopedias door to door. My income for three weeks was a promising zero. Lot of potential, though, lot of potential.

The last home I went to was occupied by a young couple with a small baby. I'm a sucker for kids. When I saw their meager surroundings I told them the last thing they needed was an encyclopedia and they should save up for the child.

So, I'm a lousy salesman. Big deal. Anyway, I beat out ten applicants at a legal publishing firm and became a "correspondent." I wrote attorneys and told them to cool it 'cause the volume they ordered was unavoidably detained in the elevator or something.

Both the correspondent next to me and myself were quick workers. She was from the coal country of Minnesota, a real doll, and we became close friends. People would often stare at us; why, I don't know, as we held hands and skipped down Market Street.

I'm all of five feet four inches tall and she was a mere five feet eleven and a half.

We'd write jokes and poems back and forth all day long. Many of these concerned life and God, since this same nagging kept intruding on my privacy. Why? What? Who? When? Huh?

Once I found myself in a serious frame of mind and wrote:

> Up above this dreary fort
> Lurks a place of last resort—
> Headed by a weird creation,
> A figment of man's imagination.
>
> "We want answers!" masses scream,
> So they receive a mystic dream—
> Super-nature in all its glory,
> Like a child's fairy story.
>
> Six days, brother, and then man,
> That is how this world began—
> So now please pray and do pretend
> We know not how this world will end.

I also carried in my wallet a definition of God which said people take all the questions they haven't discovered answers to, wrap them up into a big bundle, kick it out into space and call it "God" to ease their minds.

Man, after all, had certainly created God in his image.

In San Francisco I lived with a few guys attending San Francisco State. We had an old house in a white and black neighborhood near campus. Once in a while I'd sneak down to the corner while a black church was in session and groove on those soul-sounds pouring out into the street.

After four months in San Francisco I returned to San Diego State. At the time there was one long-haired student on campus. Most pointed to him, cracked jokes and let him sit alone in a corner of the cafeteria.

I really never dated a great deal, since I didn't particularly care for Jewish girls and the gentile chicks were heavy into their sorority scene.

I had had the misfortune of meeting Jewish girls in Los Angeles who were so wrapped up in the world of materialism that the only thing they could relate to was where daddy was going to build another home or what country they wanted to buy after graduating.

While I was still a teenager, one (she was poor) told me:

"Why, when you turn sixteen you either get a new car or a nose job!" Many get both.

The gentile chicks I met at college were on an equally bad trip. This was before the taking of drugs, let's-capture-a-building days. They held on to their image of Sally Sorority.

"Hi, there, I'm Sally Sorority! Look at my pin!" (giggles); "Oh, wow, I just love all my sisters so much!" (giggles); "Are you going to take me out tonight? Ummm? To a swingin' place? Ummm? Are we going alone?" (giggles).

"No. We're bringing your housemother."

"Oh."

Out of periodic loneliness I went a couple of times to a reform Jewish temple in San Diego. After the service I carefully nibbled on a piece of cake during the *oneg shabbat,* the social hour.

No one said hello to me.

In the summer of 1965 I was a counselor at a resident camp in Idyllwild, California, a restful mountain resort town. It was an Orthodox camp and I rather enjoyed dressing up for Friday night services and eating good Jewish chicken and matzo ball soup.

Yet, once again, it all seemed so surfacy. Nothing would reach into your guts and shake you up. Nothing from out of this world to be offered as an alternative to society's plan. Just—nothing.

When registering each semester at college we had an option as to whether we wanted to fill in the space labeled "religion." This meant if I put down "Jewish" the ethnic social group, Hillel, would be on my back all year and too many of their members reminded me of third assistant tailors from New York's garment district.

I wrote down, "Friedmanism."

"What's Friedmanism?" the girl collecting the cards would ask.

"Friedmanism," I informed her, "is the only religion which can save Jesus Christ."

I thought this very clever. A cute twist. Yet every time I said it something down deep bothered me. Bad vibes. But I ignored them.

With two years to go I still hadn't settled on a major. I flipped through the school catalogue and found out there was no language requirement for journalism majors. Whamo. I'm in.

Writing had always been my favorite hobby. I seriously thought of becoming a writer when in high school but my parents discouraged me.

"Do you know how many starving writers there are?"

I could imagine.

Yet I wanted to get through college. My father at last conceded I might be able to snag a job with a major in journalism, so didn't argue too much.

I loved it. Really far out. I even covered the student council meetings (as befits the ace reporter) and shook up the school establishment.

Each member of student government was a Greek, a frat man or sorority chick. To rub a little dirt into their neatly pressed clothes I'd show up to cover a meeting wearing bermudas, a ripped T-shirt, army fatigue jacket, bare feet and a big cigar smoking away.

If they said anything I made them look like idiots in the paper's lead story the next day. This wasn't too difficult to do.

After being graduated from good old State in June, 1967, I worked on a legal newspaper in Los Angeles for the summer. Two of my brothers-in-law are attorneys and law sounded fairly challenging.

I took the national law school admissions test, finished in the top fifteen percent and applied for law school. I felt pretty good having done so well against Harvard, Yale and the Oklahoma Military Academy.

I was accepted at a few schools, but thoughts of burying my nose into 1,000-page books for three years kept plaguing me. You know, the only dude around with white skin during the summer—Cokebottle glasses—telling Orange County residents it's time to take down their "IMPEACH EARL WARREN" signs.

I passed on law school.

My fall of 1967 was spent in Europe, including a brief visit to Israel. I went by myself, a graduation present from my Aunt Betty, but didn't enjoy the rainy days and lack of company.

In Israel I noticed smoke pouring into my room in the middle of night. Looking out the window in a half-dazed stupor, I saw flames. Sluggishly I worked my way downstairs, woke up a sleeping night clerk and asked him to quit burning garbage until the next day.

He panicked. The "garbage" was the hotel. The place was on fire!

I also picked apples on a kibbutz for a week. We'd ride out to the orchard in a one-horse cart with a grizzled old Sabra (native Israeli) in charge. The two of us sat on a make-shift car seat fastened to the flat, wooden wagon.

He turned his head to talk to one of the others riding with us and handed me the reins with no word of explanation. Hmmmm. A horse, right?

It slowed to a walk, having confirmed its suspicions that an amateur was in charge. Not wishing to be outdone I slapped the reins hard against its side and screamed.

"Eeeeeee-Yaaa!"

Va-room! It took off like a shot and nearly bounced me off. It was then I heard the only words I ever understood from this head apple-picker. He slowly turned to face me and grinned:

"Ben Hur!"

Several Israelis informed me they were the most irreligious people in the world. They were proud of it! They knew the history of the Bible, having studied it in school, but they lacked the touch of God and missed God's plan for the Jews.

This is due in part to the fact only the Orthodox branch of Judaism is recognized. The Reform and Conservative movements are not tolerated, thereby forcing energetic youngsters to shun Judaism completely rather than succumb to a rigid religious life.

My deeply implanted feelings that God, if He existed, must desire *something* from us were aroused by the negative reaction of the Israelis to any heaven-bound obligation. I admire and respect with a deep love what they have done with the land, but their souls are still desert wastes.

Back to the states. Back to the ho-hum world. Back to being a newspaper reporter.

I worked for Copley Newspapers, an extremely conservative group, for the first nine months of 1968.

Most of the time was spent with the Glendale *News-Press*.

The action of a reporter was stimulating, the slow hours were unbearable and the routine often got musty. One of our editors, Ted Mutch, had been trained through the fire of English journalism and taught me what I could never have learned in school.

As far as the community went, I was a very round peg trying to fit into a very, very square hole.

It appeared most of the town was owned and operated, if only indirectly, by church people. I'd cover one or more of their events, observe their people and conclude:

1. Christians had crew-cuts.

2. Christians always voted Republican.

3. Christians could do a lot of good, like building hospitals and orphanages, but always seemed individually detached.

4. Some Christians kept shotguns under their beds in case the Commies snuck in during the night or "those" people tried to move in next door.

The newspaper had an office in La Crescenta, in the foothills, and there worked an extremely sweet woman who admitted she believed the Bible was literally true. Man, can you believe it? Myself and another employe hassled this person without mercy, ripping her to shreds with our sarcastic tongues.

If only she could see me now.

I quit, moved to Santa Monica and decided I was a free-lance writer. By the end of the year I was desperate for a job after experiencing the *famine* part of the business without getting in on the *feast* part.

Back to newspaper work. This time for a short stint at the *Herald-Examiner.* After about five months those old fears crept back. Where ya headed, kid? Hey, man, will you die with a gold watch in your hand for thirty years' faithful service? Is *that* all life is about?

I floated from day to day. Once in a while a bottle of Scotch resting on my kitchen shelf would help me "unwind" at night after I had finished a midnight shift. Before I had a chance to change my life's direction again my city editor sent me to the Sunset Strip to find out what this evangelist was up to.

You know the rest. Bob Friedman and Jesus.

Just think. After all those years we finally met.[5]

5. Friedman, *What's a Nice Jewish Boy . . . ,* pp. 31–44.

Now test your comprehension of "Bob Friedman and Jesus" by answering the following questions:

1. Bob Friedman was born in
   a. Los Angeles
   b. San Diego
   c. Santa Monica
   d. San Francisco
2. While in grammar school he wanted to play
   a. the piano
   b. the trumpet
   c. the violin
   d. none of the above
3. He did not sing Christmas carols in the program
   a. because he had laryngitis
   b. because he refused to
   c. because he could not sing on key
   d. because he was the shortest child in the class
4. His father was a
   a. musician
   b. writer
   c. Rabbi
   d. inventor
5. They did not have a Christmas tree because
   a. they could not afford one
   b. his parents would not allow it
   c. he refused it as a pagan symbol
   d. his sister was allergic to them
6. The family celebrated
   a. all Jewish holidays
   b. only a few Jewish holidays
   c. only Christian holidays
   d. no holidays

7. The book outlining the Passover seder is the
   a. Talmud
   b. Torah
   c. Haggadah
   d. Koran
8. The author became a(n)
   a. salesman
   b. inventor
   c. journalist
   d. lawyer
9. The only branch of Judaism recognized in Israel is
   a. Reformed
   b. Conservative
   c. Orthodox
   d. Zionist
10. The author met Christ
    a. while in college
    b. while in the army
    c. while in Israel
    d. on the Sunset Strip

1. d	3. b	5. c	7. c	9. c
2. c	4. d	6. b	8. c	10. d

Continue practicing the Crosshatch while reading in your novel. Time yourself for five minutes. Enter your speed and comprehension on your record sheet.

ZIG-ZAG

Do not let this next movement scare you if your comprehension is bad. This movement should not be used for your regular, normal reading because it is designed to cut down through lines, two at a time, and not to be used on line by line reading. There are occasions when you will want to read faster than line by line, but not quite at a skimming rate. Using the **Zig-Zag** pattern run your glance on an angle from the beginning of line one to the end of line two, to the beginning of line four, to the end of line six, and so on. Doing this you will find that you will pick up large chunks of words and significant levels of comprehension. Later in the book, this pacing pattern will be used in learning effective uses of skimming and scanning. For right now this pacing pattern is a good one to use if you are simply interested in getting a quick overview of some reading material.

Practice the Zig-Zag pacing movement for several minutes. Use this pattern while reading the next article. Don't forget to time yourself and record your score.

Discipline in Morality

In 1968, a motion picture producer appearing on nationwide television made the startling prediction that the photography of sexual intercourse would be permissible in movies by 1978. His statement was thought by many to be a deliberate exaggeration—"could they ever go that far?" The producer missed his estimate by nine years; less than twelve months after the comment was made, his

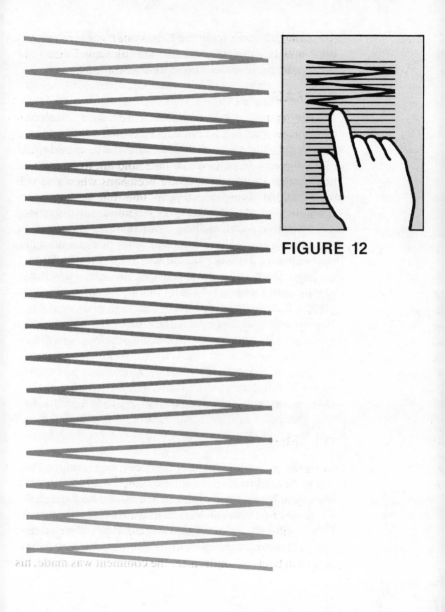

FIGURE 12

prediction became a reality in numerous motion pictures. This rapid reversal of sexual mores is unparalleled in man's history. Never has a society abandoned its concept of morality more suddenly than occurred in America during the decade of the sixties.

Although the basic ethical structure came crashing down during this brief period, the erosion of traditional morality began much earlier. The change was engineered by several key forces—each having a financial motive. Shortly after World War I, the entertainment industry discovered that considerable profit could be made by the exploitation of sex and daring new attitudes. Advertisement executives on Madison Avenue soon learned the same lesson, as did publishers and other manipulators of social opinion. Through the years they subtly undercut the importance of sexual morality, honesty, personal integrity, and meaningful faith in God. By the beginning of the sixties, Americans were wondering whether it was really so necessary to inhibit their sensual passions and impulses. "Fun and games"' looked marvelous, and after all, life was meant to be enjoyed. At this precise moment of social questioning, the Playboy Philosophy appeared with its redefinition of immorality: sexual irresponsibility suddenly became dignified and as pure as the driven snow. Believers in traditional morality were depicted as finger-wagging old hypocrites who were probably concealing a little hanky-panky of their own. After the development of penicillin (to prevent disease) and the Pill (to prevent babies), only one nagging thought inhibited widespread acceptance of the new attitude: how did God view this sexual innovation? Long ago He had threatened "Thou shalt not!" in terms that were difficult to misinterpret. This final barrier was conveniently eliminated by the theologians themselves, who announced their amazing conclusion in 1966 that "God is dead!" The way was paved for a sweeping sexual revolution which has still not reached its peak.

Not everyone in our society has allowed passion to overrule judgment. There are those who still believe, as I do, that sexual irresponsibility carries an enormous price tag for the momentary pleasure it promises. Despite the reassuring philosophy of Hugh Heffner and his Playmates, sexual "freedom" is a direct thoroughfare to disillusionment, emptiness, divorce, venereal disease, illegitimacy, and broken lives. Not only do promiscuous individuals suffer adverse consequences; history reveals that entire societies begin to deteriorate when free love reaches a position of social acceptance. This fact was first illuminated by J. D. Unwin, a British social anthropologist who spent seven years studying the births and deaths of eighty civilizations. He reported from his exhaustive research that every known culture in the world's history has followed the same sexual pattern: during its early days of existence, premarital and extramarital sexual relationships were strictly prohibited. Great creative energy was associated with this inhibition of sexual expression, causing the culture to prosper. Much later in the life of the society, its people began to rebel against the strict prohibitions, demanding the freedom to release their internal passions. As the mores weakened, the social energy abated, eventually resulting in the decay or destruction of the civilization. Dr. Unwin stated that the energy which holds a society together is sexual in nature. When a man is devoted to one woman and one family, he is motivated to build, save, protect, plan, and prosper on their behalf. However, when his sexual interests are dispersed and generalized, his effort is invested in the gratification of sensual desires. Dr. Unwin concluded: "Any human society is free either to display great energy, or to enjoy sexual freedom; the evidence is that they cannot do both for more than one generation." America is not likely to be the first to succeed in fulfilling these opposing purposes.

I have devoted the remainder of this chapter to the parents and teachers who believe in moral decency and want to instill responsible sexual attitudes in their children. Their task is not an easy one. The sexual urge is stronger during adolescence than in any other period of life, and there is no way to guarantee that an independent teen-ager will choose to control it. It is impossible, and probably undesirable, to shield him from the permissive attitudes which are prevalent today; television brings every element of the sexual revolution into the sanctuary of one's living room, and the details of immorality and perversion are readily available in the theater or from the neighborhood smut dealer. Obviously, solitary confinement of the child is not the answer. Furthermore, there is a danger that parents will make one mistake in their efforts to avoid another. While attempting to teach discipline in matters of morality, they must be careful not to inculcate unhealthy attitudes that will interfere with sexual fulfillment in future marital relations. Those who would teach this subject have the difficult responsibility of saying "sex can be wonderful" and "sex can be dangerous" in the same breath, which takes some doing. How then can conscientious adults instill self-control in their children without generating deep emotional hangups or negative attitudes? Discussed below are the aspects of sex education which are critical to the achievement of this delicate balance.

WHO SHOULD TEACH THE CHILD ABOUT SEX?

The task of forming healthy sexual attitudes and under-standings in children requires considerable skill and tact, and parents are often keenly aware of their lack of preparation for this assignment. However, for those parents who *are* able to handle the instructional process correctly, the responsibility should be retained in the home. There is a growing trend for all aspects of educa-tion to be taken from the hands of parents (or the role is deliberately forfeited by them). This is a mistake. Par-ticularly in the matter of sex education, the best approach is one that begins in early childhood and extends through the years, according to a policy of openness, frankness, and honesty. Only parents can provide this lifetime training. The child's needs for information and guidance are rarely met in one massive conversation which is typically provided by reluctant parents as their child approaches adolescence. Nor does a concentrated formal educational program outside the home offer the same advantages provided by a gradual enlightenment that begins the third or fourth year of life and reaches a culmination shortly before puberty.

Despite the desirability of sex education's being handled by highly skilled parents, one must admit that this is an idealistic objective in many homes (perhaps the majority of them). Parents are often too sexually inhib-ited to present the subject with poise, or they may lack the necessary technical knowledge of the human body. For such families which cannot, or will not, teach their children the details of human reproduction, there must be outside agencies that will assist them in this important function. Whether or not that service should be provided by the schools or some other institution depends on what will be taught in the particular program.

The issue of what to teach in formal sex education classes is of great importance to the parents who resist society's liberalized attitudes toward sex. For the children of Christian families or others with firm convictions about moral behavior, an acceptable sex education program must consist of two elements. First, the physiology of reproduction should be taught. Basic anatomy of the human body should be presented as well as the mechanics of sexual behavior in marriage. In other words, the technology of sex represents the primary content on which to focus. However, this first objective represents only half of the task. The second critical element involves the obligation to teach moral attitudes and the responsibilities related to sex. *These components should never be separated as long as the issue of morality is considered important!* Sexual sophistication without sexual responsibility is sexual disaster! To explain all the mechanics of reproduction without teaching the proper attitudes and controls is like giving a child a loaded gun without showing him how to use it. Nevertheless, this second responsibility is often omitted or minimized in the public school setting. The Supreme Court decision prohibiting prayer in schools caused teachers and administrators to be extremely self-conscious about any subject having religious overtones. They have been required to meet the least common denominator on spiritual or moral matters, meaning the subject is usually avoided altogether. Even if the ethical considerations are introduced in the classroom, they may be presented according to the concept of moral relativism. This philosophy is nothing more than a sneaky endorsement of gross immorality. According to the precepts of moral relativism, premarital sexual experiences are proper if the participants have a "meaningful relationship" going for them. Isn't that sweet? A couple can purify their sexual relationship if they can convince themselves that they like each other. Adolescents mature sexually at least four or five years before they reach emotional maturity. Thus, most fifteen-year-olds wouldn't know a "meaningful relationship" if they faced one in broad daylight. They lose all objectivity when influenced by a full moon—or a strong rock beat—or a well endowed partner. They're madly in love for at least twelve hours. Could there be any more flimsy matter on which to base an important decision than an adolescent's interpretation of love? From this viewpoint, moral relativism appears worse than a blatant recommendation of sexual promiscuity because it lends an atmosphere of pseudomorality to the behavior.

Despite their wish to avoid the issue of morality, sex education teachers find it almost impossible to remain neutral on the subject. Students will not allow them to conceal their viewpoint. "But what do you think about premarital intercourse, Mr. Burgess?" If Mr. Burgess refuses to answer this question, he has inadvertently told the students that there is no definite right or wrong involved. By not taking a stand for morality he has endorsed promiscuity. The issue appears arbitrary to his students, rendering it more likely that their intense biological desires will get satisfied.

I would like to stress the fact that I am not opposed to sex education in the public schools—provided both elements of the subject are presented properly. Simply stated, I don't want my children taught sex technology by a teacher who is either neutral or misinformed about the consequences of immorality. It would be preferable that Junior would learn his concepts in the streets than for a teacher to stand before his class, having all the dignity and authority invested in him by the school and society, and tell his impressionable students that traditional morality is either unnecessary or unhealthy. Unless the schools are prepared to take a definite position in favor of sexual responsibility (and perhaps the social climate prevents their doing so), some other agency should assist concerned parents in the provision of sex education for their children. The churches could easily provide this service for society. The YMCA, YWCA, or other social institutions might also be helpful at this point. Perhaps there is no objective that is more important to the future of our nation than the teaching of moral discipline to the most recent generation of Americans.

Let's turn our attention to other principles of sex education which parents should consider in fulfilling their important responsibility.

WHEN TO SAY WHAT

Even in this enlightened day, the subject of sex is charged with emotion. There are few thoughts which disturb Mom and Dad's tranquillity more than the vision of answering all of Junior's probing questions—particularly the ones which will get uncomfortably personal. This parental tension was apparent in the mother of nine-year-old Davie, after his family had recently moved into a new school district. Davie came home from school on the first afternoon and asked his mother point-blank: "Mom, what's sex?" The question smacked her hard; she thought she had two or three years before dealing with that issue and she was totally unprepared to field it now. Her racing mind concluded that Davie's new school must be engaged in a liberal sex education program that had introduced the subject to him, and she had no choice but to fill in the details. She sat down with her wide-eyed son, and for forty-five minutes of sheer tension she gave him a dry-mouthed, sweaty-palmed harangue about the birds and the bees and the coconut trees. When she finally finished, Davie held up his enrollment card and said, "Gee, Mom, how am I going to get all that in this little bitty square?" As Davie's mother discovered, there is a delicate art in knowing when to provide the younger generation with additional information about sex.

One of the most common mistakes committed by some parents and many overzealous educators is the trend toward teaching too-much-too-soon. In some school districts, for example, kindergarten children are shown films of animals in the act of copulation. There is no apparent gain to be harvested from plunging headlong into sex education in this fashion. In fact, available evidence indicates that there are numerous hazards involved in moving too rapidly. A child can sustain a severe emotional jolt by being exposed to realities for which he is not prepared. Furthermore, it is unwise to place the youngster on an informational timetable that will result in full sophistication too early in life. If an eight-year-old boy is given an advanced understanding of mature sexual behavior, it is less likely that he will wait ten or twelve years to apply his knowledge within the confines of marriage. Another danger resulting from premature instruction involves the threat of overstimulation. A child can be tantalized by what he is taught about the exciting world of grown-up sexual experience. Childhood should be devoted to childish interests—not adult pleasures and desires. I am not implying that sex education should be delayed until childhood has passed. Rather, it seems appropriate that the amount of information a youngster is given should coincide with his social and physical requirement for that awareness.

The child's requests for information provide the best guide to his readiness for sex education. His comments reveal what he is thinking about and the facts he wants to know. His questions also offer a natural vehicle for instruction. It is far better for his parents to answer these questions at the moment of curiosity than to ignore or evade them, hoping to explain later. Premeditated training sessions often become lengthy, one-way conversations which make both participants uncomfortable. Although the question-answering approach to sex education is usually superior, the technique is obviously inadequate for use with children who never ask for information. Some boys and girls are fascinated by sexual reproduction while others never give it a second thought. If a child is uninterested in the subject of sex, the parent is not relieved of his responsibility by the absence of questions. The use of small animals, as described in the following section, is an excellent way to generate the necessary curiosity.

One final comment is important regarding the timing of sex education in the home. Parents should plan to end their instructional program immediately before the child enters puberty (the time of rapid sexual development in early adolescence). Puberty usually begins between ten and seventeen years of age for girls and between twelve and nineteen for boys. Once they enter this developmental period, they are typically embarrassed by discussions of sex with their parents. Adolescents usually resent adult intrusion during this time, preferring to have the subject of sex ignored in the home. We should respect their wish. We are given ten or twelve years to provide the proper understanding of human sexuality; after that foundation has been constructed, we can only serve as resources to whom the child can turn if he chooses.

ASSISTANCE FROM MOTHER NATURE

As indicated above, small animals can be very helpful in the process of sex education. I can think of no better audio-visual aid than a pregnant cat who is not sensitive about being observed. The subject of reproduction can be gracefully presented after an animal has demonstrated the process of birth. I heard of a seven-year-old boy who left his mother this note: "Dear Mom. Our poor kitty came all apart in the garidge today. Love, Richard." Mom rushed out to the "garidge" to find that the cat had given birth to six little kittens. She and Richard held an important conversation that evening about kitties and babies and such things. This natural introduction to sexual reproduction was inevitable for children raised on farms, but city children often experience nothing more helpful than an abstract explanation. I would recommend that parents get their children a prolific pet. If Dad just can't stand cats, then dogs, hamsters, or any other mammals can be of assistance.[6]

6. Dr. James Dobson, *Dare to Discipline* (Glendale, California: G/L Publications and Tyndale House Publishers, 1970), pp. 159–168.

Now test your comprehension of "Discipline in Morality" by answering the following questions:

1. In 1968 a motion picture producer predicted that by 1978
    a. complete nudity would be permitted in movies
    b. sexual intercourse would be permitted in movies
    c. movie trends would become more conservative

2. The entertainment industry discovered that considerable profit could be made by the exploitation of sex and daring new attitudes
    a. shortly before World War II
    b. shortly after World War II
    c. shortly before World War I
    d. shortly after World War I

3. Advertisement executives, publishers and other manipulators of public social opinion subtly undercut
    a. the importance of sexual morality
    b. honesty
    c. meaningful faith in God
    d. all of the above

4. The final barrier to the widespread acceptance of the new morality was eliminated by
    a. penicillin
    b. the Pill
    c. "God is dead" theology

5. The sexual urge is stronger during
    a. adulthood
    b. adolescence
    c. childhood

6. Ideally, sex education should originate
   a. in the church
   b. in good books on the subject
   c. in the home
   d. in grade school sex education classes
7. As long as morality is an important issue, _____ and _____ cannot be separated
   a. sexual desire and marriage
   b. love and moral values
   c. technology of sex and sexual responsibility
   d. anatomy and sexual psychology
8. Adolescents
   a. mature sexually before emotionally
   b. are realistic about sexual responsibility
   c. have an innate sense of good behavior
   d. none of the above
9. Sexual education ideally
   a. should follow a well-planned schedule
   b. should prepare a young child to be ready for his coming sexual experience
   c. should be purely factual
   d. coincide with the child's social and physical development
10. Sex education in the home should
   a. end just before puberty begins
   b. continue during the teen years
   c. never become a time of embarrassment
   d. follow a common pattern for all children in the family

| 1. b | 3. d | 5. b | 7. c | 9. d |
| 2. d | 4. c | 6. c | 8. a | 10. a |

Now time yourself as you use the Zig-Zag movement in your novel. Record your score as usual. How much do you remember of the contents after reading in this manner?

SPIRAL

The next movement will be a welcome change for it is the most natural of the pacing movements and therefore easiest to do. Simply pace across the line, turning down at the end of the line, making a return sweep that brings you back up under the next line you wish to read. Practice this **Spiral** pacing motion for several minutes in your novel. When you feel ready, practice it on the following article. Time yourself for five minutes so you can compare your rate for the Spiral with other movements.

"Stuttering Stephen"

One man . . . one life . . . one work—and the great American West was changed. ETHEL BARRETT *tells a stirring story based on the life of*

Stephen Paxson, the boy nobody wanted, who became the greatest Sunday School missionary in the history of America.

Once upon a time back in the early 1800's right here in mid-west America, lived a boy whose mother gave him away. His name was Stevie Paxson.

His mother was a widow, and the only way she could see that her children were provided for was to farm them out to make their own way. She farmed Stevie out to a man named Harmen Fagen.

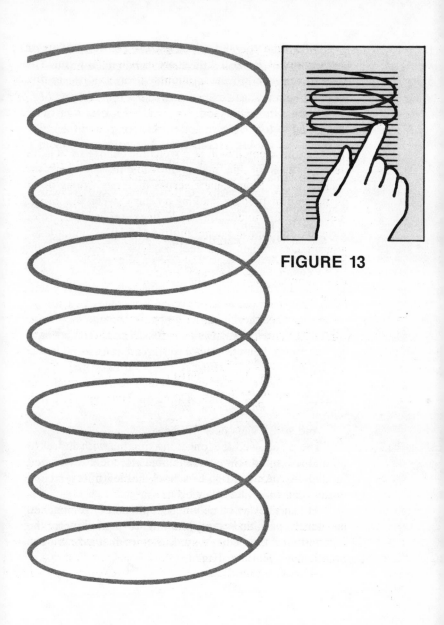

FIGURE 13

Stevie was frozen with fear when old Harmen took him to his farm, whoa'd the horse, and called out to his wife: "Euphemia! Euphemia, come out and see the boy!" And Euphemia Fagen came bustling out the kitchen door.

"Well, Stevie Paxson!" she said, looking him over from head to toe. "We've got a room for you in the attic. Harmen, get his grips. And when fall comes . . . What's the matter? Cat got your tongue?"

"No ma'am. I—I stammer, ma'am."

"Oh, my land. Ain't that too bad. And its worse when you're scared? Like a square knot in your belly?"

"Y-yes, ma'am."

"And you're scared now?" Euphemia could see he was.

"Yes, ma'am."

"Well, never mind," Euphemia reached up to help him down from the buggy. "When fall comes you can go to school. Teacher'll learn you how to talk. And you can . . . Harmen, don't look so cross. The agreement said we had to send him to school for three months—no less!"

"And no more!" Harmen glared at his wife.

"Well, no less. Stevie, you can learn to read and write and talk in that time. Come on, Harmen. Help him with his grips."

And so Stevie's new life began.

There followed the long, long summer with chores to do and rows and rows of vegetables to hoe. Stevie lived for the day he would go to school and learn to read and write—and talk, like other boys.

At last the day came when Euphemia Fagen packed his lunch pail and sent him off to school with the admonition, "Don't be scared, Stevie. Just take a deep breath and speak up. Hm?"

"Y-yes, ma'am."

And so Stevie started down by the south pasture where the gate was busted, through the short-cut toward that wonderful school yard. The biggest adventure of his life began . . . . . . and ended.

By the time Stevie reached school he was so scared he couldn't open his mouth. The other children made fun of him, and the teacher was a cold impatient man with no time for boys who couldn't talk. Before Stevie knew what was happening the teacher packed him off for home with a note saying he wasn't about to teach Stevie to read until first someone taught him to talk.

And Stevie's big adventure was over before it began.

Harmen Fagen was no help. "Don't care if he can't read," he said, glancing over the note. "Long as he can work, it don't matter."

It turned out that it didn't matter. Stevie couldn't have gone to school anyhow. He got something called white fever. His leg was horribly swollen—his fever was high—he was desperately ill. Euphemia used to read to him in the evenings.

"Are you awake, Stevie?"

"Yes, ma'am."

"Does it hurt?"

"Awful, ma'am."

"Well I got a nice book—it'll make you forget. It's about a Quaker preacher." And she would settle down on the bed and begin to read. "Once upon a time there was a Quaker preacher who went about doin' good."

A Quaker preacher who went about doing good. All through Stevie's recovery he thought about that. And he thought, "If God would ever let me walk again I'd go about doing good, good, gooder than even that Quaker preacher."

Well, God did let Stevie walk again, but with a limp. He was no longer of any use to Harmen Fagen. And so Stevie left Harmen and Euphemia to become an apprentice to a hatter in a town farther west. He remained there for a year. And there he discovered things about himself—about his own personality. Traits—abilities—weapons for living.

He discovered he could learn to read. By asking! He plagued his colleagues and learned his letters from signs and newspapers. And he taught himself to read—at least the small words.

He discovered too that he had rare gifts from God. A sunny disposition for one thing. He was the brunt of all the jokes. Everyone called him stammering Stephen. But he had an elasticity—he could spring back up! He was learning the laws of survival.

And he discovered that he could sing! The traveling salesmen dropped in the hatter's shop with their guitars and sang ballads. Steve had a voice like a silver trumpet. And when he sang—he didn't stammer! Like Euphemia had said—singing untied the square knot in his stomach. He was free!

In those years Steve learned from a human standpoint the secret of living. He migrated a little farther west and set up a hatter's business of his own.

And then he met and married Sarah. It was a real love match—a good marriage. Two children blessed their home—first Mary, and then little John. It was a good life.

But that boyhood vow kept echoing in Steve's mind. "If God would make me walk again," he had said, "I'd do good, good, gooder than even that Quaker preacher."

Well, he limped. But he was walking. And he did do good. His hatter's business was successful. He fiddled for the Saturday night square dances. He was the best liked man in town. A good husband and father. A happy, useful man. And then. . . .

Jesus Christ stepped into Stephen Paxson's life and said, "I am God." Life could be even better.

For Steve Paxson was soon to feel the impact of a great work. Like a giant hand, the American Sunday School Union was reaching out to the west and organizing Sunday Schools. Its goal was a Sunday School in every new community, and its missionaries worked tirelessly to achieve that goal. One of these missionaries was the Reverend John Peck, who had established a Sunday School in the town where Steve Paxson lived. And through this small Sunday School God began to work.

It started one Sunday at dinner when Steve asked his little daughter Mary, "Well, what did you do in Sunday School today, Mary?"

"I learned some verses. And we marched. And sang. Oh! And we're having a contest, papa. We're to bring new scholars. And if I bring one I get a star!"

"Well, that sounds fine. I hope you get your scholar, Mary."

"Oh, I will, papa." Mary's eyes danced with excitement. "I'm going to try real hard!"

But Mary didn't get her scholar. All that week she tried without success, and the next Sunday morning Mary made one last try.

"I didn't get one, papa. And I won't get my star." She was standing on a chair waiting for him to finish buttoning her dress.

"I'm sorry, dear." Steve fumbled with one of the buttons. He had an idea what was coming.

"Papa, would you be my scholar?"

"I'm . . . not that sorry, Mary."

"Papa—please!" Her little-girl charm was wearing him down and she knew it. "So I can get my star?"

"Mary . . . I . . . don't tease me like that." He finished buttoning the last two buttons, stalling for time. "Tell you what I'll do. I'll walk down with you . . . and wave my hand in the door . . . so you can get your star. Then I'll be on my way."

And that's how it happened that tall Steve Paxson and little Mary Paxson went down to the Sunday School that had been started by the American Sunday School Union.

The service had already begun when they got there and Mary pleaded with him to come inside—"so I can get my star!" And if that wasn't bad enough, once inside the door Steve ran headlong into Mr. Willis, the superintendent.

Steve *said* he was just there to look around, but before he knew what was happening Mr. Willis introduced him to a class of boys and asked him to teach. Mr. Willis begged, the boys pleaded, and Steve was ready to run!

"Fellows. I can't. I can't read well enough."

"That's all right, Mr. Paxson. We'll help you with the hard words." The boys weren't going to take "No" for an answer! "Yeah, Mr. Paxson. You tell us everything you know, and we'll tell you everything we know."

"That's . . . what I'm afraid of." But suddenly it seemed like a *good* idea. And on impulse, he made up his mind to take the plunge—a strange plunge, it was, into a new adventure.

It was a struggle all the way through. First there was the lesson, with the boys helping out on the "big words." Then he had to ask questions out of a book. After that he had to hear their memory verses. Verse after verse after verse. Steve was amazed at how much they knew. And a spark within him began to glow.

And when class was over . . . "Will you come back next Sunday, Mr. Paxson? Please?" A roomful of eyes looked up at him, pleading.

"I . . . well, I'll tell you, fellas. I'll come back if we can do this same lesson again. And next week I'll be pre . . . I'll be prep . . . I'll study!"

Stephen Paxson was on fire!

He went back the next Sunday. And every Sunday for four years afterward. He did visitation until that little Sunday School was bursting at the seams! And some time during those four years he turned his whole life over to God. He asked Christ to be his Saviour.

During those four years, Steve kept asking God to help him talk. And one day, he discovered that he really could talk. The secret was exactly what Euphemia had told him all those years before. Just take a deep breath . . . and . . . "Sarah" he burst out. It was his first complete sentence without stammering. "I'm going to be a Sunday School missionary."

"Why Steve—you *can* talk! You said a whole sentence without—you're going to be a *what?*"

Yes, Steve had made up his mind. He was going to be a Sunday School missionary!

The need was great. With headquarters in Philadelphia, the Sunday School Union was the greatest movement in the history of the young nation. They were putting Sunday Schools all over the Mississippi Valley, but the towns were popping up faster than the missionaries could keep up with them.

So Steve sold his business and together with the children he and Sarah migrated to the Mississippi Valley. It wasn't easy. They built their own crude log cabin and

Sarah was left alone with the children much of the time—with blankets over the doors and windows, and the wolves and coyotes howling outside at night. Some nights they were so close. Once after Sarah had blown out the candles she felt something in bed with her. With trembling hand she lighted the candle. It was the watch dog! He had jumped in bed for protection!

So Steve Paxson became an American Sunday School Union missionary, limping up and down the Mississippi Valley, establishing Sunday Schools wherever he went. Later, when he had a buggy, he and his horse went from town to town talking to folk and inviting them to Sunday School.

"Do you know Jesus died for sinners?" Steve would ask, stopping his horse and buggy beside a group of children.

"No, sir. Ain't nobody 'round here died for sinners. Leastways if he did I ain't heard tell of it."

"I mean the Son of God. Do you know God?" and Steve would invite them all to Sunday School. "We'll meet in back of the grocery store. I'll teach you to read and sing and all about Jesus."

Stephen Paxson established 1,314 Union Sunday Schools, and helped reach 83,000 children for God. The Sunday Schools flourished, developed into churches, and spread as the West spread. God alone knows of the Christian families—the pastors—the missionaries—the repercussions of the work of one man with two great handicaps. Neither handicap stopped him. The limp . . . .

. . . or the stammer. For the most amazing thing about Steve Paxson's life was that stammer. When he was sent back east to be (of all things!) a speaker, the newspapers revealed the final evidence of God's hand in his life.

They raved! They said he was the finest orator of his time! He had a magnetic control of an audience . . . and a voice like a silver trumpet! God had taken his greatest weakness and made it his greatest strength.

One man—with great odds against him. One life—dedicated to God. One work—spreading like a prairie fire across the great American West. This was Steve Paxson—a living demonstration of what God can do with a man whose life is yielded to Him.[7]

7. Ethel Barrett, "Stuttering Stephen," *Teach* magazine, Spring Quarter 1967 (Glendale, California: G/L Publications, 1966).

Now test your comprehension of "Stuttering Stephen" by answering the following questions:

1. Stephen Paxson went to live with the Fagens because
      a. his parents were dead
      b. it was closer to the school
      c. his mother was a widow and could not provide for them
      d. he was crippled

2. Stevie was sent home from school
      a. for being disobedient
      b. because he couldn't talk
      c. for fighting with another student
      d. because he had white fever

3. Stevie's vow to God was made on the basis
      a. that his stammering stop
      b. that he walk again
      c. that he learn to read
      d. that he could go back to school

4. Stevie left the farm
      a. to be close to a doctor
      b. because he couldn't work in the fields anymore
      c. because the hatter wanted a son
      d. to return home to his mother

5. Stevie's stammering disappeared when
      a. he talked in his sleep
      b. he got married
      c. a teacher gave him speech lessons
      d. he sang

6. Steve went to Sunday School because
      a. there he could sing in the church choir too
      b. his daughter begged him to go

       c. he didn't want Sarah to go alone
       d. the pastor especially invited him
7. Steve's first unstammering sentence was
       a. "Praise the Lord!"
       b. to his Sunday School class
       c. a vow to become a Sunday School missionary
       d. a vow to be a better father
8. The Paxson family moved to
       a. the Mississippi Valley
       b. the Ohio Valley
       c. southern Arkansas
       d. North Dakota
9. Steve's voice
       a. finally gave out entirely
       b. became his greatest asset
       c. was never very pleasant
       d. was called "smooth as silk"
10. Steve Paxson started _____ Sunday Schools
       a. 827
       b. 3000
       c. 1314
       d. 2222

1. c	3. b	5. d	7. c	9. b
2. b	4. b	6. b	8. a	10. c

HOP

You are now ready to learn your last pacing motion, the **Hop**. It is particularly effective because it emphasizes seeing groups of words at one fixation, rather than seeing individual words. It is also rhythmical and very fast. In this movement, instead of sliding your finger under each line, you are to **point once at each half of the line.**

As you read, this pointing quickly takes on a hopping motion as you raise and lower your eyes on each group of words. If you find that you are missing some words with two jumps per line, you may wish to practice the motion by hopping three times per line. Now Hop your way through the next reading selection. Be sure to record your reading score when you are done. And if you haven't yet entered on your record sheet the rate from your last reading drill, do so now.

Mud, Mosquitoes
and Miracles

One mile north of the famous 'Six Flags Over Texas" amusement park in the Dallas suburb of Arlington, Explo's "Tent City" division of approximately 2,000 delegates bivouacked for the historic week.

"Camper's Corral," some twelve acres owned by Pat and Jean Hall and located about twenty minutes west of Dallas, suddenly blossomed on Sunday afternoon into a colorful assortment of campers, tents, mobile homes and house trailers. Two huge circus tents were erected to accommodate the training sessions. The size of the acreage had to be tripled.

Casual elements of the Jesus people brought little more than bedroll and Bible for quarters under the stars.

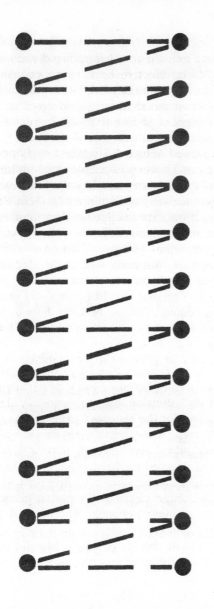

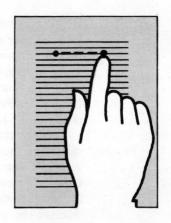

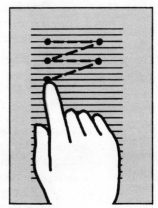

FIGURE 14

The motto for campers willing to endure the spartan fare for fifty cents per night was introduced early and accepted by all: "God can't make it rough enough to make me complain." Before the week had hardly begun the subscribers to that motto were in store for a severe test of their willingness to stand by their Tent City declaration.

Long lines queued before the outdoor registration tables that first day as hundreds of people stood for hours in a field with no shade. Many people were transferring from other conferences to attend the one at Tent City. Directors had to set up a special line for these transfers. The heat became almost unbearable.

For that first meeting in Camper's Corral, the directors sensed the need for a speaker who could effectively communicate to a wide spectrum of personalities. Jack Sparks, head of the Christian World Liberation Front in Berkeley, was scheduled but he became ill two days before Explo. All other speakers were tied up. Things looked pretty bleak.

The staff began to pray. Still they could find no teacher for the opening sessions. Then God's providential circumstances took over. Billy Graham came for a casual visit and stayed to preach. He challenged the delegates to a devoted walk with the Lord. The Tent City conference was on its way!

A few minutes after Dr. Graham left, a bolt of lightning split the sky, followed by angry sheets of driving rain. The violent storm continued until half an inch of bone-chilling precipitation had turned the hard ground into a morass.

The construction workers who put up the two large tents had warned that the dry ground had been so hard it broke their pile driver and they couldn't sink the stakes as deep as they should have been driven.

"If it rains," they said, "the stakes may come loose and pull up, letting the tent fall."

The staff could barely shout above the thundering rain. Warren Willis from Berkeley explained the situation to the crowd. The delegates began to sing.

"Praise the Lord!" they shouted above the thunder.

Gary Speckman advised the staff to pray and ask the Lord what they should do. As they prayed silently for God to reveal His will the only other sound was the rain on the thin, canvas roof.

"After about twenty seconds more of rain the storm began to slacken," Gary recalled. "In a ten-second period it changed from a downpour to a drizzle. Suddenly a tremendous cheer arose from the group. We had met our first big problem and conquered by trusting."

The camp was a far cry from the running water and room service of downtown hotels, but there were no complaints and the lessons in patience added to the spiritual experience.

Two nights that week many delegates returning from the Cotton Bowl discovered that storms had blown down their tents, soaking everything including the contents of many a suitcase.

"We don't know why it had to happen, Lord, but we love You anyway," sighed Explo delegate Les Bartell as he wrung out his sleeping bag.

Gary walked through the camp one night at about midnight, helping where he could. Many of the delegates were singing and laughing as they re-set their tents. One guy asked if anyone had seen the Ark.

"It got waterlogged and sank," someone called back.

On Thursday night, when the rainstorm soaked the Cotton Bowl audience, Tent Citians were stopped by policemen at the entrance and informed that many would have to find outside housing that night. Somehow citizens in the area had already discovered the plight of the Explo delegates. Within half an hour approximately 500 people evacuated from Camper's Corral were warm and comfortable in private homes. They all left with the promise that they would be back in time for the 7 A.M. meeting.

The spiritual lessons of Tent City abounded.

"I realized how I had taken everything for granted," a girl testified, "—the right to be clean, to have hot showers, enough sleep. . . ." When at the end of the week she finally took a shower at a friend's house it was a special kind of blessing she had never experienced.

"If a tent was good enough for Abraham, it's good enough for me!" Camp Director Paul Lewis exclaimed.

Another camper admitted: "I reached my level of tolerance on the second day, only to find things still being washed out in a second rain. But I found that God gave me the strength to carry on in a joyful manner."

This camper found it "easy to begin to get angry with God," but he discovered release in repenting and asking God to forgive.

A bedraggled camper spreading wet clothes over a car to dry saw a purpose in the twin rainstorms. "I believe God dumped rain on us to bring us into a closer fellowship with Him," he said. "I believe He wanted total commitment in any situation—not just something that we liked."

Still other testimonies were wrung from the mud:

"I thank God for the tremendous and pervading spirit at Tent City. It seemed whatever was thrown at the people they rejoiced. . . ."

"During the stressing times and urgent moments I still had time to minister to others on the camp grounds. . . ."

"I appreciate the opportunity I had to work with other staff teams, submitting to others placed in authority over me. It was not always easy to do things their way because I did not always understand them."

Director Lewis announced to the staff that week, "They're saying down at Explo headquarters that this is an impossibility and that we are the ones God has chosen out of 3,000 staff members to live and work in this 'impossible' situation."

A coed testified: "This is the first time I've ever had to trust God for my physical body and physical conditions beyond my endurance. It has taken me beyond the point of trust I've had before."

On the printed activity sheet for Tent City the top line read: "6 A.M. Rise and greet the Son." That spirit carried the delegates through the sticky heat of that slough of despond. It would have been pretty tough to sleep anyway after the Eschatos took the mike and shook the camp with reveille in gospel songs.

"Through the week of Explo," a girl staff member recalled, "as I got less and less sleep (from five hours to three hours at the end of the week) I saw God demonstrate a supernatural patience and a ministering by His Spirit inside me. I always wanted to come back and serve more after I'd finished my assigned chores. This was demonstrated among the kids, too, such a *giving* spirit as only God our Father has."

The absence of credit to individuals was noted. It was always, "Jesus in the morning, Jesus at noon, Jesus till the sun goes down!"

At certain hours of the day the acreage resembled a

monastery—young people in humble garb sitting cross-legged on the grass studying. These same people became spirited worshipers under the tent when general assemblies were called.

One day a business man from the local McDonald's stand visited camp with several hundred coupons for free cheeseburgers. The staff limited the coupons to kids who really needed them. On another day a local farmer gave the settlers sixty dozens of eggs. "I heard you might need them down here," he said. A nearby gas station manager offered fillups at two cents per gallon off the regular price and 20 per cent off for repairs.

A woman testified: "I had almost given up on young people, but you kids have restored my hope for the future."

A bus driver set up a canvas-covered kitchen and dispensed free coffee during one of those rainy nights after delegates had returned from the Cotton Bowl.

When it wasn't raining it was boiling hot. Afternoons were especially tiresome. There were only 29 showers and 14 sinks to accommodate 2,000 people on those 38 acres. Sessions were moved to 7 A.M. to get a head start on the heat.

The Irving Fire Department brought a hydrant wrench one afternoon and an old fire hose. Delegates set up a "fountain" and several hundred ran for their swim suits.

Most of the staff at Tent City had to stay up all night for at least one night. Everyone had to pull together to make the program work.

"We learned quickly how to love each other," Gary said. "In effect, we were responsible for setting up a small community for one week. It required establishing a sanitation system, a police force, a city government, food distribution, a hospital, a phone and message service, a post office, bookstore, transportation system, and garbage control. Oh, yes, we also held a training conference."

Delegates at Tent City said it often: The most significant aspect of the entire conference was the *expressed* unity of Christ's body. The more difficulties they faced together the more clearly they became one in the spirit.

This attitude prevailed on the final night when a staff member announced to the group that a van belonging to one of the delegates had clutch trouble requiring $80 for repairs. He asked those willing to help to come to the platform and put money into an envelope.

After the meeting was over people filed up in a steady stream to put money into the envelope. Quickly the total was reached and an announcement told the people to stop giving. But the next day some were still trying to give money to help.

On Sunday morning, one week after the first delegates had arrived at Camper's Corral, the staff shared experiences with Pat and Jean Hall at breakfast. Many of those nights the Halls had been up at all hours. They had shared the hard times as well as the blessings. The Halls did a complete 180-degree turn in their estimation of the living God by the end of the week. Pat's a rough, husky man but he had tears in his eyes as he said, "I now believe in the Lord, because of the integrity of your kids. We really loved having you here. Any time you can come back, please stop in."

Jean later told a newsman as she looked out over the camp, "They're beautiful people. They behave so well. It's nice to have some guests for a change who don't complain. Some folks could take a lesson from these people."

Ezekiel 36:23 can be appropriately applied to the six days of mud, mosquitoes and miracles: "Then the nations will know that I am the Lord, when I prove myself holy among you in their sight."[8]

8. Paul Eshleman, *The Explo Story* (Glendale, California: G/L Publications, 1972), pp. 71–77.

Now test your comprehension of "Mud, Mosquitoes and Miracles" by answering the following questions:

1. The fire department
   - a. put out a fire in the main tent
   - b. provided water for campers to clean up
   - c. rescued a pet cat in a tree
   - d. revived those overcome by heat
2. During the six days Pat and Jean Hall
   - a. objected to the noise
   - b. cooked for the campers
   - c. accepted the Lord
   - d. got angry at Gary over sanitary arrangements
3. Billy Graham
   - a. was the scheduled speaker at Tent City
   - b. preached on the Second Coming of Christ
   - c. gave an evangelistic challenge
   - d. challenged them to a devoted walk with God
4. The first rainstorm did not
   - a. bring down the big tents
   - b. make too much mud
   - c. test the patience of the campers
   - d. cease when the campers prayed
5. Problems of Tent City included
   - a. overcrowding
   - b. lack of hot showers
   - c. ants
   - d. drugs in camp
6. An unexpected pleasure occurred when
   - a. the sun dried up some of the mud
   - b. Tent Citians got to sleep in

c. a local restaurant sent chicken dinners for everyone

d. spent a night in private homes

7. The mood at the close of Tent City was

    a. relief that the ordeal was over

    b. unity among the body of believers

    c. a rush that caused a traffic jam

    d. depression over the week of discomfort

8. A description of the six days was

    a. heat, helping, heaven

    b. mud, mosquitoes and miracles

    c. mud, mosquitoes and mire

    d. fellowship, friendship and trust

9. The various difficulties caused the campers to

    a. become irritable and quarrelsome

    trust more and more in the Lord

    c. leave camp two days early

    d. recognize how much the Explo staff was doing for them

10. The campers rejoiced over

    a. several who accepted the Lord

    b. the heat and mud and physical difficulties

    c. the daily inspirational sessions

    d. the many new friends they made

1. b	3. d	5. b	7. b	9. b
2. c	4. a	6. d	8. b	10. c

For more practice using this motion, take a five-minute reading drill in your novel, doing the Hop. Record the results when you are done.

Things worth remembering are worth repeating. Since the Hop is a good pacing motion to remember and since most people find that it is the most efficient pacing movement, use it again, this time on the next reading selection. And don't forget to record your score.

Sign of the White Carnation

Father had tried to smuggle his own money out of the country with a man traveling from Germany to Holland. All of our private funds had been confiscated. When you left Germany, you left everything. He wanted to have a few marks waiting for us if we made it to Holland.

The Germans found my father's name and address in the man's pocket and picked father up. At this time it was an honor and not a disgrace for a Jewish man to be imprisoned.

Then rumors circulated that a young Jewish boy had killed a German. Supposedly, this led to the violent mob reaction which roared through the city on November 9, 1938.

November 9. The day they burned all the synagogues. And Jewish centers. And every business with a "JEW-ISH STORE" sign in the window. Screaming, fiercely yelling out anti-Semitic slogans, the gentile civilians made it a real family affair. Including my former play-mate, Alfred!

A highly organized mass of adults and youth threw bricks, stones, chunks of pavement—anything—through windows, at well-stocked shelves and trembling owners. They were very thorough. It went on for a good twenty-four hours. I huddled in our apartment and listened to hundreds of bottles being smashed at the corner drugstore. We could hear everything from where we lived and my imagination soon filled in details of unseen destruction.

My mother was away with Marga when it started. I paced along a thin path stomped into the rug. Back and forth, back and forth. Emmi, our housekeeper, accused me of imitating a lion in a cage. It was really happening. There was nothing you could do about it. Nervously I feared something terrible had happened to mother. Later, a turn of the front door knob—and I knew mother was safe.

The shock of this unexpected attack was not as great as the sinking feeling which numbed the merchants as they helplessly watched a life's work being systematically destroyed. You couldn't resist. You couldn't fight. You couldn't get help.

If we had lived in a ghetto like Warsaw perhaps we could have mustered strength as a unit. But we were too scattered for that in Berlin. We were easily divided and conquered. The sadness hit me immediately when I went outside the next day after most of the mob had dispersed.

I was walking briskly to an English lesson when I passed the drugstore. For a fraction of a second I glanced at the owner's face as he stared with blank eyes at children tossing in a few more rocks for good measure. I'll never forget it.

Utter helplessness. Agony brought to a sharp peak and then leveling off into a narrow road which leads to no future but which you must keep moving upon. No recourse. No police protection. No civilian help. The entire world against you, and you but half a man.

Mother promptly sold our furniture, pictures and

anything else which would raise money for our illegal passage into Holland. We needed several thousand dollars. The money was finally collected and arrangements made with those men now in this type of business.

Wednesday, December 1, 1938, father was released on parole with instructions to report to his board the following Monday. Trouble was already gathering momentum for the weekend when we heard another wave of persecution would hit the Jews.

We told Emmi we would be gone for a couple of days. We were not worried about her telling on us, for she was a dear friend, but it was better she didn't know for her own protection. Later, when she was questioned, she could honestly say she didn't know we were leaving.

Emmi, in a demonstration of loyalty to our family, would rip apart the many summons she received to attend nationalistic meetings. Before we left she came to me and said, "Please, you aren't going to leave without telling me, are you?"

Thursday I was told we would be trying to go across the border and to take anything I wished. The entire idea of this type of adventure tickled my fifteen-year-old fancy. It was very exciting.

At once I dug deep into a pile of family photographs and began to pick the ones I liked best. My parents wondered how, of all things, I could choose photographs. But over the years they were very grateful.

Friday morning I called Marion. I was a perfect actress as I casually said I wanted to know how she was and so forth. No one was permitted to know of our plans, yet I didn't want Marion to say I never called.

Friday afternoon, luggage in hand, we left our apartment and walked down the street. A few blocks passed under foot before a car pulled to the side and picked us up. Driving all day, becoming lost in a strange mixture of anxiety and hope, we finally reached the border town of Aachen at midnight.

It was too late to make an attempt that night. We sneaked to the rear of an inn and tiptoed to a few rooms in the back. Up front, in the restaurant, German soldiers were loudly drinking and laughing away the evening.

Late the next afternoon we boarded a train at a small station, with instructions to get off at a tiny community where a man wearing a white carnation in his lapel would meet us. Television drama takes a poor second to real life circumstances.

He was waiting. We all piled into his car and as he drove he explained a play-by-play plan of what we were to do at a remote soccer field.

The night became deadly black with no lights or stars to illumine our path. We quietly stopped the car at this open field located in swampy country directly on the German-Holland border.

He pointed to a near set of goal posts. Our starting point. Then his finger stretched a little and indicated another set of posts across the field—not quite as far apart as those on an American football gridiron. Our finishing point.

We merely had to run from one set of goals across the field to the other and wait for a Dutchman to go "tch, tch, tch" in the night. At this point we'd slip into Holland and the whole family would have scored.

Somehow the other side missed the point. We grabbed our things and sloshed across the field, waiting patiently under the far posts, straining our ears for the sound of "tch, tch, tch."

It never came. We were severely warned not to try

to make it by ourselves, for the swamps were extremely dangerous. The driver advised us to simply wait.

Which we did. Minute after painful minute. We stood facing each other, mother and father, Marga and myself. The driver had also instructed us what to say in case we were caught so he wouldn't get into trouble. He assured us it was "99 percent" safe.

Standing there in the freezing night I kept dwelling on that one percent he hadn't included. A good *yiddisha* mind.

For two hours we didn't say a word and subdued our breathing to minimum volume. We hid our faces as much as possible so a passing patrol wouldn't throw any light off of our shiny skin.

As soon as my feet were planted in a semi-permanent position I began to pray. I continued the entire time in prayer, silently, strictly between me and God.

I promised God everything under the sun if He'd somehow get us out. For years my parents had taken me from one doctor to the next in a vain attempt to help me grow. I told God I didn't care anymore if I grew—just so we'd be free. (This was very important and for years afterwards I was hesitant about seeing a doctor for fear I would be breaking my promise to God.)

I finally whispered to father, begging him to return to Germany. "It's better to be in Germany, and healthy, than in Holland with pneumonia!"

"Shhh!"

I really didn't understand the circumstances, of course. Cold and hunger had taken the sharpness from my reasoning powers. I simply knew I was miserable with nowhere to go.

At last father decided to go back. No one was going

to come for us. Our legs ached as we headed through the rain toward the other side of the field. Then . . .

"Stop or I'll shoot!"

The heavy voice stabbed the silence of the night and pierced the eerie quietness. What was happening? Caught? *Hey, father! Father!*

He started running. What could he be thinking? Trying to outrace a bullet? Once more the voice cried out.

"Stop or I'll shoot!"

"Father, come back! Father, don't . . . come back!" We screamed after him and he stopped in his tracks, slowly turned and walked back to his family. We searched each other's faces before peering up at our captor.

It was the Gestapo.[9]

9. Vera Schlamm, *Pursued* (Glendale, California: G/L Publications, 1972), pp. 33–39.

Now test your comprehension of "Sign of the White Carnation" by answering the following questions:

1. The author's father was imprisoned for
    a. being a Jew
    b. trying to escape from Germany
    c. smuggling stolen goods
    d. trying to smuggle his own money out of the country
2. The violent mob reaction of November 9, 1938 was supposedly triggered by
    a. orders by the German high command
    b. fear of the high Jewish population
    c. a young Jewish boy had killed a German
    d. fear of a Jewish organization
3. The mob of violent Germans
    a. burned synagogues and Jewish centers
    b. shouted anti-Semitic slogans
    c. threw stones at windows and shopkeepers
    d. all of the above
4. The Jews could not resist or fight back because
    a. there were too few of them in Berlin
    b. they were too scattered to be effective
    c. they were too frightened
    d. they were mostly old people
5. They did not tell Emmi where they were going
    a. because she might try to stop them
    b. because they were afraid she might tell
    c. for her own protection
    d. because she was going along
6. The things she decided to take along were
    a. her baseball
    b. favorite books

        c. family photographs

        d. family heirlooms

7. The escape involved traveling by

        a. car

        b. foot

        c. train

        d. all of the above

8. The last leg of the journey was across

        a. a swamp

        b. a soccer field

        c. a football field

9. The family waited for their Dutch guide

        a. only a few minutes

        b. two hours

        c. several hours

10. For years her parents had taken her from one doctor to another

        a. for an allergy condition

        b. for asthma

        c. in an attempt to help her grow

        d. for birth defects

1. d	3. d	5. c	7. d	9. b
2. c	4. b	6. c	8. b	10. c

WHICH PATTERN DO YOU LIKE?

Now that you have tried all nine pacing patterns, is one pattern better for you than another? Why do you feel this pattern helps you read faster? After practicing all of the new motions, especially work on the one or two pacing motions with which you feel most comfortable. For further improvement of your reading skills, consider the following suggestions:

1. Use each new technique you learn on the explanations and discussions of rapid reading in this guide. New skills can only be effective if you use them.
2. Besides using your reading skills on light reading such as novels, apply rapid-reading techniques to all your outside reading. This includes correspondence, newspapers, magazines and anything else that you normally read during a day.
3. More important than anything else, is to set aside a specific time period every day for practicing your rapid reading. Thirty minutes of daily rapid-reading practice is enough to insure steady progress. Although any reading material will do, it is best to begin with easy material and gradually work up to a more difficult level.

Remember, always use a pacing pattern when you read. By the way, did you pace while reading this page?

154

5

READING GROUPS OF WORDS
SPAN OF PERCEPTION

In the following section you will overcome word-by-word reading and learn instead how to see large groups of words. This skill is learned in several stages, all of which should be carefully considered:

1. Space Reading
2. Circling
3. Slashing
4. Grouper Card
5. Eye Stretching
6. Eye Swing

But before we get to these six stages, let's see how the eyes work.

SPAN OF PERCEPTION—FIXATIONS

Many people hinder themselves from using their full reading potential because they use their eyes inefficiently. Their span of perception is very short because they only see one or two syllables per fixation, instead of learning to perceive phrases from two to four words at a single glance. The following illustrates a poor reader's perception pattern:

Mr. Barbing sat in his rocking chair thinking about

his childhood. It didn't seem possible that the years

had passed so quickly. He could still remember his

high school days when he had squirted the ink from

his inkwell across the classroom with his quill.

College was only a flashing memory. Even the many

years he had put in with the firm no longer seemed significant. Life had passed too quickly.

A fixation, or a point at which the eyes stop, is represented by each dot, while the arc indicates the span of perception for that point. To see the span of perception for an efficient reader, note the following:

A good reader's span of perception should be like the following:

Mr. Barbing sat in his rocking chair thinking about his childhood. It didn't seem possible that the years had passed so quickly. He could still remember his high school days when he had squirted the ink from his inkwell across the classroom with his quill. College was only a flashing memory. Even the many years he had put in with the firm no longer seemed significant. Life had passed too quickly.

Now look back over the perception pattern on this page. Try to see each phrase with one glance. Focus your eyes on the dot instead of directly looking at the words.

SPAN OF PERCEPTION—FIXATION PARAGRAPH

Before you can get into the "hows" of fixation or learn to do any of them, you need to know exactly how much you can take in per fixation right now. This next exercise will help you measure your present span of perception. You will need a partner in order to do it, so ask someone to assist you. It can be a horrible experience if you get the wrong person. But on the other hand, this fixation exercise has been the beginning of many lasting friendships.

First of all, take the AGP Fixation Card provided in this book. It is the card with two paragraphs on it and a hole in the center. Have your partner hold the card to his nose with the print side out and look through that hole at your eyes. Now, ignoring that blue eye staring through at you, read the first paragraph aloud.

Why aloud? Because if we read silently, we are apt to cheat. We know there is someone looking through the card at us, and because we want to make a favorable impression on the other person, we tend not to fixate as often as we normally would. Instead, we glaze our eyes a little bit and sweep over the card without really reading. When you read aloud, you can't bluff. It will cause you to read slower, but you will still have the same fixation span. That part doesn't change; you simply spend a little bit longer on each span.

Now as you read, have your partner watch your eye movements. He will see your eyes move across the lines in a series of quick jerks called fixations. His job is to count the average number of fixations per line as you read. Then take the card yourself and, looking through it, count your partner's eye fixations as he reads the second paragraph aloud to you.

While you are counting, both of you will see that eyes don't really flow while reading. Rather, they move along the line in a series of small jerks almost like a typewriter and then—ding—back to the beginning of the next line. They jerk across the line again, and then once more back to the beginning.

You saw the tendency of the eyes to stop and jerk. But did you also notice some kind of regression? Did you also notice that the speed of fixation varies; that sometimes the eye seems to stay longer on certain words than on others? This is where pacing comes in. With our pacing exercises, we are trying to even out your speed of perception, to keep you from spending too much time on some words and teach you to get a rhythmic movement across the line.

Now, how did you and your partner do in this fixation exercise? How representative were you? The average person takes in 5/8″ or about five to seven characters per fixation. The lines of type on the card are six inches long. So if you are representative, you probably took in five to seven fixations per line. If you averaged six fixations per line, that means you are taking in approximately one inch per fixation. If you averaged fewer than five to seven fixations, your eye span is better than average. To measure your progress in grouping as you continue rapid reading, periodically use the Fixation Card.

READ ABOVE THE LINE

Now you will practice the first exercise in building an increased span of perception: **Space Reading.** In order for you to stop focusing on individual words and to encourage you to "broaden" your perception to take in groups of words, it is important that you learn to "read above the line." Try to develop this new skill by looking only at the dot above each phrase on the page below. You will be able to see the phrase without looking directly at it. Practice Space Reading the following phrases at least ten times.

●
The log cabin

●
lay hidden

●
so that

●
lived quietly

●
the humdrum

●
If ever

●
the couple

●
within this quaint

●
you would

●
your problems

●
as frightening

●
surrounded by shrubs

●
from human view

●
its inhabitants

●
away from

●
of rushing society

●
you met

●
that lived

●
little log cabin

●
undoubtedly feel

●
were not really

●
as you thought

Now take any page in your novel, dot all the phrases (any group of words that look like they go together) and practice Space Reading it. Try putting the dots in every two words at first, and then after a few lines like this put in dots for every three words, and continue this "stretching" until you are attempting to see each line in a maximum of three phrases. After you feel you can comfortably do this, try Space Reading without dots, looking into the space directly above the phrase you are trying to see.

One word of caution. Don't expect to practice phrase reading for only a few minutes and then have mastered the technique. Daily practice is required if you are to "stretch" your normal span of perceptions. Ten minutes a day spent practicing grouping drills is a good investment.

CIRCLING

So that reading phrases instead of individual words becomes natural to you, we are providing you with a **Circling** exercise.

In the following paragraph while using a pacing pattern look at the circles instead of the words. Practice reading phrase after phrase as fast as you can until your eyes relax and feel comfortable in seeing words in groups.

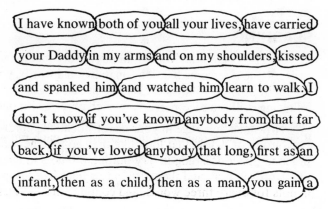

I have known both of you all your lives, have carried your Daddy in my arms and on my shoulders, kissed and spanked him and watched him learn to walk. I don't know if you've known anybody from that far back, if you've loved anybody that long, first as an infant, then as a child, then as a man, you gain a

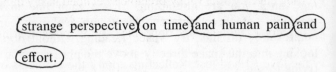

strange perspective on time and human pain and effort.

Now go back over the material you have already read in this guide and choose a passage and divide the words into meaningful phrases by Circling them. The phrases don't have to be grammatically correct units, but should be one-half inch to two inches long.

Circle phrases for approximately ten minutes. Then practice focusing your eyes on the circles, hopping your eyes from one circle to the next. Repeat this exercise until your eyes become a little more adept at taking in phrases. The repetition will gradually accustom you to **think** groups of words, as well as to **physically see** groups.

Begin Circling.

(**Note:** Don't begin any other drills until you are certain that you are beginning to read groups of words. If you feel you are not able to read in phrases at all, go back to the beginning of span of perception instruction and start over.)

SLASHING

If you are beginning to feel that you are no longer struggling to overcome fixations on individual words, you are ready for the following exercise in **Slashing.** On the following drill practice perceiving each phrase with only one glance. Each new phrase is separated by a slash. Remember, use a pacing motion to point at each phrase and look above the phrase, not directly at it.

The thunderous roar / of crashing waves / upon / the

jutting edge / of the rocky precipice / echoed in my mind / as I stood / alone on the opposing / shore / remembering / the love / I had lost. Reflecting upon / the moments of joy / I had shared / in the past, my cold / and shivering body / became intoxicated / with the warmth of memory. / Even if / there was a storm, / I could see / the calm rising / of a restful dawn.

Repeat this exercise at least ten times before continuing. The repetition causes monotony; the monotomy will cause you to relax and thus perceive phrases a little easier. Once you are in the **habit** of looking for groups, rather than looking for individual words, half the grouping battle is won.

THE GROUPER CARD

An advanced **Grouper Card** is provided for you. Its purpose is twofold: to increase speed and span of perception, and to develop efficient eye-swing movements. After you cut it out, follow the instructions printed on it and practice reading with it on your novel or other printed materials. Using the Grouper Card will help you see more words at a glance and decrease the time it takes for you to see words, thus dramatically increasing your reading speed. If all you do is learn to see two words at a time instead of the one word you normally see at each fixation, your speed will double and you will have better comprehension. The two-hole part of the Grouper Card will help you to develop efficient eye swing. If you practice daily for only a few minutes, you'll see definite progress in only a few weeks.

Using any reading material, take your Grouper Card and begin to read.

Place the grouper at the top of the page. Slide it straight down the center of the page as fast as possible, reading the groups of words centered in the slit. As your eyes are able to take in the words at a glance, widen the slit a quarter-of-an-inch at a time and repeat the drill. This drill is especially effective when used with a newspaper column.

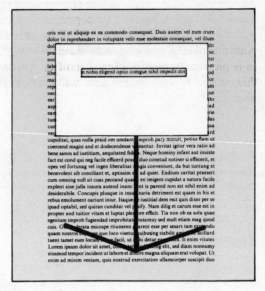

EYE "STRETCHING"

With proper training, your eyes may be able to see and comprehend common print phrases up to two inches in length. The following exercises will provide you with such training so that your perception of phrases will be "stretched," enabling you to increase your present grouping abilities.

Exercise 1

In the illustration below, the object is to read each line of numbers by focusing only on the dot in the middle of the line. Using a separate sheet of paper, write down the numbers you perceive in each line as you focus ONLY on the dot. Do not look at the numbers directly. You will discover that each time you repeat the exercise, you will see more numbers on each side of the dot. Practice until your peripheral vision comprehends as much of the line as is physically possible for you (after you have repeated this exercise five times you will probably be at your physical limits).

Begin. . . .

```
9 8 5 2 8 5 4 0 1 · 0   7   5 4 8 6 2 8 2
1 4 7 0 9 7 4 2 0 · 7   4   1 2 9 0 8 4 3
0 8 9 6 7 4 2 3 0 · 1   7   0 5 3 7 9 8 3
8 6 4 8 0 3 2 1 8 · 0   1   4 2 6 8 4 2 9
9 7 5 0 8 8 3 5 7 · 7   4   9 8 2 2 4 8 0
7 8 4 7 5 3 9 0 2 · 0   7   3 5 1 4 9 0 6
2 3 5 4 6 9 9 6 1 · 9   9   7 4 5 3 4 9 0
0 9 7 6 4 3 7 6 5 · 9   5   3 3 1 4 7 8 6
8 7 4 9 8 4 2 3 4 · 9   6   4 2 7 5 3 8 0
5 8 7 3 1 4 6 8 0 · 4   9   6 4 3 2 6 8 0
5 7 8 9 4 7 6 3 1 · 7   8   9 0 8 5 3 2 6
0 8 6 4 2 1 3 4 6 · 3   2   7 8 9 8 6 4 2
8 6 4 3 2 5 4 8 9 · 7   5   4 7 6 8 9 0 3
8 6 4 8 0 3 2 1 8 · 0   1   4 2 6 8 4 2 9
9 7 5 0 8 8 3 5 7 · 7   4   9 8 2 2 4 8 0
7 8 4 7 5 3 9 0 2 · 0   7   3 5 1 4 9 0 6
2 3 5 4 6 9 9 6 1 · 9   9   7 4 5 3 4 9 0
```

Exercise 2

Now focus your eyes on letters instead of numbers, and repeat the exercise, again looking only on the dots. You will quickly see that letters are easier to see for most people than numbers.

```
Q W S C F T Y H N · K O L B K U Y G V
X F G B H U J N M · O L M Y T F C D E
P I U Y R E W Q A · D F G H J K L M N
L K J H G F D S A · X C V B N M P O I
Z X C V B N M A S · F G H J K L O I U
H G F D V C X Z Q · E R O I U Y H J K
L P O K M N J I U · B V G Y T F C X D
R E S Z A W Q A Z · W E D C F T Y H N
Z A Q S X C D W E · V B G R T H N M J
M J Y U I K L O P · I Y T R E W Q A S
W E R T Y U I O K · H G F D S X C V B
Q W S C F T Y H N · K O L B K U Y G V
X F G B H U J N M · O L M Y T F C D E
P I U Y R E W Q A · D F G H J K L M N
L K J H G F D S A · X C V B N M P O I
Z X C V B N M A S · F G H J K L O I U
H G F D V C X Z Q · E R O I U Y H J K
L P O K M N J I U · B V G Y T F C X D
R E S Z A W Q A Z · W E D C F T Y H N
Z A Q S X C D W E · V B G R T H N M J
M J Y U I K L O P · I Y T R E W Q A S
W E R T Y U I O K · H G F D S X C V B
```

Exercise 3

For something a little more challenging, try the following exercise which contains symbols that may be difficult to duplicate. Try to duplicate the symbols on a separate sheet of paper looking only at the center line.

```
1 2 3 4 5 6 7 8 9 │ 1 2 3 4 5 6 7 8 9
! # " $ % _ & ' (  │ ' & _ ) : ? , * @
* ) ' & % $ # " !  │ @ : + ) ' & % $ #
/ ¢ ' & % & ( ) *  │ $ " ! # % & ( * '
! & ) ' _ $ ' # %  │ ( * + @ ? ! $ _ (
@ + * ) ' & % $ #  │ # $ % & ( * + ! :
; ¢ / = / ¢ ( & %  │ _ ' / ! ; ¢ = - :
* + & % $ # _ ' (  │ ? @ % " ! # % $ &
. ? @ # ) ' _ % $  │ " _ ' ) * + @ . ?
_ $ # " $ % _ & (  │ + : . , ! # " % '
& & % $ ( * @ $ /  │ ¢ = - . , / 0 & $
1 2 3 4 5 6 7 8 9 │ 1 2 3 4 5 6 7 8 9
! # " $ % _ & ' (  │ ' & _ ) : ? , * @
* ) ' & % $ # " !  │ @ : + ) ' & % $ #
/ ¢ ' & % & ( ) *  │ $ " ! # % & ( * '
! & ) ' _ $ ' # %  │ ( * + @ ? ! $ _ (
@ + * ) ' & % $ #  │ # $ % & ( * + ! :
; ¢ / = / ¢ ( & %  │ _ ' / ! ; ¢ = - :
* + & % $ # _ ' (  │ ? @ % " ! # % $ &
. ? @ # ) ' _ % $  │ " _ ' ) * + @ . ?
_ $ # " $ % _ & (  │ + : . , ! # " % '
& & % $ ( * @ $ /  │ ¢ = - . , / 0 & $
```

Exercise 4

Swing your eyes from cluster to cluster at a steady pace. Since you are looking at numbers and letters instead of blocks, go slowly enough to comprehend what is there. After glancing at a couple of lines, take a sheet of paper and write down the exact letters and numbers you have just read. Repeat this ten times.

ddddd ⟶	IIIIII
FFFFFF ◄━━━━►	9999999999
4444	eeeeee
vvvvvvv	mmmmmmm
TTTTTTT	ZZZZZZ
kkkkkk	55555555
8888888888	QQQQQQQQQ
ggggggg	ooooooo
WWWWWWW	7777
aaaaaaaaa	AAA
YYYYYYY	xxxxxx
nnnnnnnn	PPPPPPPPP
111111111111	wwwwwwwww
jjjjjjjjjjjjjj	tttt
HHHHHHHH	222222
vvvvvvv	mmmmmmm
TTTTTTT	ZZZZZZ
kkkkkk	55555555
8888888888	QQQQQQQQQ
ggggggg	ooooooo
WWWWWWW	7777
aaaaaaaaa	AAA
YYYYYYY	xxxxxx
nnnnnnnn	PPPPPPPPP
111111111111	wwwwwwwww

Exercise 5

Now apply your new reading technique on phrases using the pacing movement as you read. The object of the exercise is to achieve a smooth, flowing return sweep while perceiving each phrase before moving on to the next phrase.

Now try practicing rhythmic reading on a passage in your novel. Spend five or ten minutes concentrating on hopping your eyes with a smooth motion. Make certain that you use a pacing motion.

The conductor's conscience	opined
a fairyland	with turkey
seemingly	persistent
like a rachet	Archaic design
maybe	a sword shining bright
pointed	hateful
highway engineer	at the fringe
he scratched his ear	from protogalaxy
a blood curdling	coupon
The sexton's	railroad
"Huzzah!" was all	a grand style
the daffodil's sway	of Buffalo, New York.
The Curse of the Elephant	curbed
a coat of many colors	replac-
ed his pancakes	belatedly
of course	while filming
highway engineer	at the fringe
he scratched his ear	from protogalaxy
a blood curdling	coupon
The sexton's	railroad
"Huzzah!" was all .	a grand style
the daffodil's sway	of Buffalo, New York.

6

VOCALIZING AND ITS CURES

Vocalizing is one of the habits that takes away from the effectiveness of the acceleration and grouping techniques you have learned. This chapter will explain how you can overcome this habit.

I remember the first course I ever taught. There was a fellow sitting in the front row in the corner who was a severe vocalizer. In fact he was so bad that during the first three-minute reading I wandered over and watched him read. He vocalized so much that he whispered when he read—he actually made a little bit of noise even though he was reading silently.

At the end of the three-minute reading, his speed was 125 words per minute. Well, obviously I couldn't do much for him with a rapid-reading course. In fact I complicated his reading a little bit because he needed remedial help rather than rapid-reading help. By the end of the three-week session his speed had gone from 125 words per minute down to 90 words per minute.

But this is an extreme case. Most people do not vocalize to that degree, and in fact, can fairly easily cure their vocalizing.

Should you be one of the many people who have vocalizing difficulties, those who move their lips, tongue or even whisper the words that they are reading, be sure to try the cures suggested: mumble-reading, humming, chewing gum or touching lips. These cures are also effective for determining if you have a vocalizing problem. If you are unable to do easily the following four things while reading, you have a vocalizing problem to some degree and ought to practice these cures every day for a few minutes until you find that you no longer vocalize.

Mumble-reading involves repeating aloud a meaningless phrase such as "1-2-3," "1-2-3" or "mumbo-jumbo," "mumbo-jumbo" while at the same time reading silently. You will quickly find that it is physically impossible to vocalize and mumble-read at the same time. If you keep mumble-reading you will find that your habit of vocalizing will be broken because you are forcing yourself to say something other than what is being read.

Humming involves the humming of a simple tune as you read silently. Since this forces the lips to be pressed together most of the time, it is especially effective for people who find they are lip-movers. This keeps the lip-mover from silently forming the word as he reads.

Chewing gum is an easy exercise and very effective. Chew several (three or more) sticks of gum at the same time and with a rhythmic, cud-chewing motion. This will involve all parts of your mouth in guiding the gum, swallowing the juices, and will make it very difficult for you to chew and still vocalize while you are reading.

Touching lips simply requires you to place your fingers lightly on your lips as you read silently. Any lip-moving will be obvious and you can then make yourself doubly conscious of it by pressing slightly on your lips each time you catch yourself vocalizing.

Remember: vocalizing is a habit and like all habits is correctable as long as you make yourself aware of it when you catch yourself vocalizing.

Now turn to any section you have already read, and practice one of the suggested cures for several minutes.

Begin practice. . . .

7

TECHNIQUES FOR INCREASED EFFICIENCY

COMPREHENSION BUILDING

There are essentially two main ways to build comprehension:

1. Question **before** reading. You must always be conscious of comprehension as you read and this can best be accomplished by reading with a questioning mind. We have all been in situations, perhaps even in Sunday School classes where we have been asked to read specific pages in preparation for the next class. And we did the reading. But at the next class when we were questioned on the contents of those pages, it seemed that we didn't know much.

Has this happened to you? Sure.

But, how different it was those few times that the teacher asked us to read specific pages, but also indicated what it was that we should look for: "Discover the route that Paul took on his first missionary journey." "Who were the people that he came in contact with?" "What were the theological issues that he touched on?" And so on.

What difference did it make when you were questioned the next class? A tremendous difference! You knew three times as much as you previously knew.

What was the difference? You were reading with a questioning mind. You were reading with a purpose, and not just passively passing your eyes over pages. Awareness of your purpose tells you when you can skim and when you can safely skip things altogether.

You must raise questions about your reading material **before** you begin reading. What do you want to get from your reading? What do you want to know? What is the thesis or problem here? What is the purpose of this work? What is the main sequence of ideas? What particular things will you be hunting for in this work? By raising questions like these before you read, when you come across the answers they will stand out, and they will be remembered.

2. Preview and postview. If you will preview quickly the material you are about to read—that is, take a couple minutes to glance briefly at each page (using an Arrow or Zig-Zag pattern) before reading—you will get an overview of the contents in terms of main ideas, thesis, style, significant illustrations, etc., which will give greater understanding of the material when read. The effect of this is to give you a feeling of confidence and assurance, thus increasing speed and comprehension. You feel as if you are covering familiar territory. This pre-reading also enables you to discard useless material without wasting time reading it for detail.

Pre-reading is also an essential step in defining your precise purpose in reading a particular work. Pre-reading will also indicate when the content is familiar, is irrelevant to your purpose, or too technical for you to handle, and thus can be safely skipped.

This previewing and then reading should always be followed by **postviewing** of the material. Postviewing is simply previewing **after** you have finished reading, and its purpose is to note for a second time the important points that were covered during the reading. The rapid review of the contents in just a minute or two will reinforce the key points and main issues of the reading and will aid retention.

You can become the world's fastest reader, but if you don't know what you have read, your rapid-reading skill will be of no use to you. So that you will be able to read faster and maintain good comprehension, we will encourage you to develop the habit of skimming (one way of previewing) and scanning after you read, which will give you an overview of the material and a broader understanding of key points. The techniques of skimming and scanning are covered next.

There is a confusion in terms here. Most people when speaking of skimming and scanning—and even skipping—are talking about the same thing. But these terms do have different meanings.

SKIMMING

Skimming is defined as reading unfamiliar material, looking for main ideas. When you skim you rapidly perceive **the main ideas** of a book, chapter, report or article instead of reading the material from beginning to end. But Skimming involves more than just lightly passing your eyes over the pages in hopes that something is going to hit you.

So how do you skim? Develop the habit of **rapidly reading the first sentence** of each paragraph which is nearly always the topic sentence (the sentence which spells out the most important point in the paragraph). This will enable you to have a basic understanding of the important ideas in the work, at a speed five or six times as fast as you normally could read the material. As you rush through the work Skimming, don't allow yourself to read the details of any paragraphs, only topic sentences. You are reading for ideas now, not details.

Time yourself as you skim your next reading selection in this book. Immediately after you finish reading, write down the main idea of the article in a few sentences before answering the comprehension questions following the exercise.

Discipline Gone to Pot

There is no more certain destroyer of self-discipline and self-control than the abusive use of drugs. The teen-ager who has begun taking narcotics often shows a sudden disinterest in everything that formerly challenged him. His school work is ignored and his hobbies are forgotten. His personal appearance becomes sloppy and dirty. He refuses to carry responsibility and he avoids the activities that would cause him to expend effort. His relationship with his parents deteriorates rapidly and he suddenly terminates many of his lifelong friendships. The young drug user is clearly marching to a new set of drums—and disaster often awaits him at the end of the trail.

During 1967 and early 1968, I served as a consultant for a federal narcotics project in a large metropolitan area. Part of my responsibility was to conduct psychological evaluations for thirty-two former addicts who were being trained to help current users. Even though these ex-addicts had supposedly ended their narcotics habit, each of their lives reflected the immeasurable human tragedy imposed by drug abuse. Several of the men had first been arrested during their early teens and subsequently circulated in and out of prison for more than thirty years. Most of them had endured extreme poverty and hardship during their youth. Each man described his own pathetic childhood, involving broken homes, parental alcoholism, severe beatings, and loss of loved ones. The typical example which follows was taken from the written evaluation of Floyd, a 27-year-old Caucasian who had spent seventeen years in prison.

"In the hour before Floyd's appointment, another subject was being evaluated, yet Floyd broke into the room without knocking. It was immediately apparent that he had interrupted something important, but he offered no apology. He wore a dirty, stretched T-shirt and an old Russian hat, and his hair was disheveled. Later during his testing session, he belched loudly but offered no comment. He spoke without tact or social grace. The examiner's first reaction was one of irritation and rejection. However, as the testing session progressed and Floyd's background unfolded, the events in his childhood so totally explained his present behavior that acceptance and compassion replaced the revulsion. Floyd was a child who was hopelessly doomed by fate. His father was an alcoholic whose drinking kept the family in utter poverty. Floyd had four sisters, and the family endured the same hardship typically experienced in impoverished alcoholic homes. But Floyd's situation worsened significantly when he was seven years old. His mother departed with another man, leaving the five children without fanfare or notice. The children were left in the 'care' of their alcoholic father who was completely unqualified for the responsibility. The needy youngsters were forced to lean on each other—they had no one else. This situation existed through the remainder of Floyd's childhood and adolescence. He had no guidance, no religious training, no social instruction, and no love. He bears the deep psychological scars from the lack of parental concern. He has grown like a wild weed—uncultivated, undisciplined, and unappreciated.

When he entered school, Floyd felt dirty, ragged, and inadequate. He had a few friends and he fought regularly. To compound matters, he developed a difficult reading problem. Consequently, he felt foolish and out of place in school. All through the elementary and junior high school years he experienced the daily ego assaults of school failure and social ridicule. He hated high school even more intensely. When he reached the legal dropout age, he immediately quit school. It is not surprising that narcotics and lawlessness appealed to him."

Another man in the project, named Phil, described his experience with heroin—the most dangerous of all drugs and the one which is now being used by teen-agers in epidemic proportions.

"I was arrested for stealing a car when I was thirteen and sent to a reform school until I was fourteen. I got hooked on heroin right away and my parents kicked me out of the house; I've been on my own ever since. One year later I was arrested again and sent off for two and one-half years. When I was released I was immediately involved in all kinds of burglaries, including a pharmacy robbery. I was arrested for that offense and put in prison for another year, and I was free only a few hours before I was back on heroin again. I was out of prison for three weeks and then sent back for another term. This cycle went on for fourteen years. I've now been out only five months, but this is the first time I've stayed clean.

I was hooked worse after the last time I was released. I had an unending supply of heroin because I was selling the stuff. By that time I had a common-law relationship with a girl, and she built up the same habit. She worked as a prostitute to make enough money to support her habit. It was costing us $20.00 each just to go to sleep at night. Every five hours we had to have a fix. We were stealing everything that wasn't nailed down. We were always sick. We started leaning on each other, telling each other that 'it's going to be all right.' For the first time in my life I felt something for somebody else; I let the barricade down for the first time. I let myself care for someone. Then we were arrested for armed robbery and forced to go through withdrawal symptoms. I took the kick episode terribly. I was so badly hooked that I hemorrhaged inside. My wife tried to commit suicide. We were both delirious. The first thing I remember is the doctor yelling at me, 'You're going to die, you're going to die—who's your next of kin?' I can't remember anything more. I made up my mind, however, that I wasn't going to die. I began to recuperate and I did much thinking. After I got out of prison this last May I found my common-law wife again and she had started using narcotics again. I told her to stop or forget it this time. She would not give up her heroin and so our relationship ended. It caused me great emotional pain to cut her out of my life. She's in San Francisco now; she just got out of prison and I'm sure she's using heroin again."

Examiner: "Do you have any regrets?"
Phil: "Drugs were my means of survival."

While it is not surprising that Floyd and Phil turned to narcotics as a convenient escape from their difficulties, the motivation of many affluent teen-agers is much less apparent. It is not unusual for a middle or upper class adolescent to become addicted to harmful drugs, even though he lived in a home where love and goodness abounded. This tragedy occurs at all levels of society; no child is immune to the threat—neither yours nor mine. Every parent must inform himself of the facts regarding drug abuse. We should be able to recognize its symptoms and stand prepared to guide our children should the need arise. The remainder of this chapter is devoted to a brief review of the essential information parents should know about narcotics and drug abuse. Though some of the facts are technical, it is recommended that the reader learn or even memorize the important details from this summary.

WHAT ARE THE SYMPTOMS OF DRUG ABUSE?

At the beginning of this chapter I mentioned several of the attitudinal and behavioral characteristics of individuals who are using harmful drugs. Listed below are eight related physical and emotional symptoms that may indicate drug abuse by your child.

1. Inflammation of the eyelids and nose is common. The pupils of the eyes are either very wide or very small, depending on the kind of drugs internalized.
2. The extremes of energy may be represented. Either the individual is sluggish, gloomy, and withdrawn, or he may be loud, hysterical, and jumpy.
3. The appetite is extreme—either very great or very poor. Weight loss may occur.
4. The personality suddenly changes; the individual may become irritable, inattentive, and confused, or aggressive, suspicious, and explosive.
5. Body and breath odor is often bad. Cleanliness is generally ignored.
6. The digestive system may be upset—diarrhea, nausea and vomiting may occur. Headaches and double vision are also common. Other signs of

physical deterioration may include change in skin tone and body stance.

7. Needle marks on the body, usually appearing on the arms, are an important symptom. These punctures sometimes get infected and appear as sores and boils.

8. Moral values often crumble and are replaced by new, way-out ideas and values.

Each drug produces its own unique symptoms; thus, the above list is not specific to a particular substance. If the parent suspects that his teen-ager is using narcotics or dangerous drugs, it is suggested that the family physician be consulted immediately.

WHERE ARE THE DRUGS OBTAINED?

Illicit drugs are surprisingly easy to obtain by adolescents. The family medicine cabinet usually offers a handy stockpile of prescription drugs, cough medicines, tranquilizers, sleeping pills, reducing aids, and pain killers. Furthermore, a physician can be tricked into prescribing the desired drugs; a reasonably intelligent person can learn from a medical text the symptoms of diseases which are usually treated with the drug he wants. Prescriptions can also be forged and passed at local pharmacies. Some drugs reach the "street market" after having been stolen from pharmacies, doctors' offices or manufacturers' warehouses. However, the vast majority of drugs are smuggled into this country —perhaps after being manufactured here and sold abroad. It is estimated that eight billion doses of dangerous drugs are manufactured annually in the United States, and approximately half of these reach the black market.

HOW MUCH DO NARCOTICS COST?

Though the prices of various illicit drugs vary, the following figures represent the approximate black market values for the substances indicated at the present time:

1. Amphetamines: 10 cents per pill.
2. Methamphetamine: $3.00 to $5.00 per small paper package (one injection).
3. Barbiturates: 20 cents per pill.
4. Marijuana cigarettes: 50 cents each.
5. Heroin: $2.50 to $5.00 per capsule (one injection). Within a few months' time, the cost of heroin usage can range from $20.00 to $200.00 a day.

WHY DO THE KIDS DO IT?

If we are to help adolescents avoid the tragedy of drug abuse, we must understand the typical circumstances surrounding initial decisions to experiment with narcotics. It is not generally true that unscrupulous "pushers" give teen-agers their first dose. Rather, the introduction to drug usage is usually made from friend to friend in a social atmosphere. Marijuana and pills are frequently distributed at parties where a nonuser cannot refuse to participate without appearing square and unsophisticated. Many teen-agers would literally risk their lives if they thought their peer group demanded them to do so, and this need for social approval is instrumental in the initiation of most drug habits.[10]

10. Dobson, *Dare to Discipline,* pp. 183–189.

Now, as you were instructed at the beginning of "Discipline Gone to Pot," write down the main idea in a few sentences. Then go on to answer the following questions and record your results.

Now test your comprehension of "Discipline Gone to Pot" by answering the following questions:

1. There is no more certain destroyer of self-discipline and self-control than
    a. abusive use of alcohol
    b. promiscuous sex
    c. abusive use of drugs
2. The writer of this article was responsible for _____ in the federal narcotics project
    a. physical examinations
    b. psychiatric examinations
    c. psychological evaluations
    d. sociological evaluations
3. The childhood of many of those interviewed had involved
    a. well-to-do parents
    b. abundant parental love and concern
    c. parental alcoholism
    d. sufficient discipline
4. Floyd and his four sisters were left in the care of his alcoholic father when
    a. his mother died
    b. his mother was arrested
    c. his mother left with another man
    d. his mother went to visit her sister
5. The most dangerous of all drugs and the one which is now being used by teen-agers in epidemic proportions is

    a. marijuana
    b. heroin
    c. barbiturates
    d. amphetamines

6. Some symptoms of drug abuse are
    a. nausea
    b. headaches
    c. double vision
    d. all of the above

7. It is not unusual to find drug abuse
    a. among lower class adolescents
    b. among middle class adolescents
    c. among upper class adolescents
    d. all of the above

8. Approximately _____ percent of the 8 billion doses of dangerous drugs produced annually in the United States reach the black market.
    a. 25%
    b. 35%
    c. 50%
    d. 75%

9. Within a few months' time the cost of heroin usage can range from _____ to _____ a day.
    a. $5–$10
    b. $2.50–$5.00
    c. $10–$50
    d. $20–$200

10. The introduction to drug usage is usually made
    a. by an unscrupulous "pusher"
    b. on a dare
    c. in a social atmosphere

1. c	3. c	5. b	7. d	9. d
2. c	4. c	6. d	8. c	10. c

Now to find out how correct you were in finding the main idea, go back and rapidly read the article again using your choice of pacing pattern. Time yourself and enter your speed on your record sheet.

SCANNING

Scanning is defined as reading familiar material, looking for facts or details.

If you are reading for details, the scanning technique will be a great aid to you. It will allow you to quickly find specific points, or to locate facts and figures to support an idea. Scanning is like skimming in its visual gliding through reading material. Yet, it is different in two ways: first it helps the reader find information that he already knows is in the work (because he has already read the material). Secondly, the reader must know what he is looking for.

You will find that items you are looking for seem to stand out at you as you scan. Any items concealed in a paragraph—such as dates, titles, key words, places, vocabulary, and technical facts—can easily be found by scanning. Simply run your eyes in diagonal lines from the first word in a paragraph to the middle line of the paragraph at the right margin and then back to the beginning of the second paragraph. Repeat this technique for each paragraph.

Using a time limit of not more than two minutes, scan the selection upon which you practiced Skimming. Pick out significant words and details and ignore sentences.

Remember: Skimming is the previewing technique which allows you to get an overview of the main ideas that are covered in the material. Scanning is the postviewing technique which enables you to find details and helps you remember specific points.

From now on always preview and postview everything you read, both in this course and on your outside reading. Spend at least twenty seconds previewing and the same amount of time postviewing each reading selection as you practice. Also, make certain that you always preview and postview reading matter that is part of your everyday reading.

Since you will want to adapt Skimming and Scanning to your reading needs, feel free to experiment with these techniques.

Enter your speed and comprehension for the last selection on your record sheet and compare this score with all the others you have listed. Has your rapid reading progressively improved? Don't be discouraged if your score seems to be jumping up and down. That often happens when you are first learning to read faster. The general trend on your record sheet should be moving gradually up the chart.

A METHOD FOR MARKING MATERIAL

Most of us like to read with a pen in our hand so that we can mark important ideas or facts as we come to them. This combination of reading and marking is an aid to our comprehension because it serves to focus our attention on what we are reading. The problem with reading like this is that few of us learn a system for marking materials and thus fall into a habit of simply underlining everything. Reviewing material that we have marked this way is quite complicated because we must re-read everything in order to find out the relative importance of the marked material. To avoid this, learn the following marking system and use it whenever you read. The result will be an improved and speeded-up organization and review of material read.

For major concepts such as a thesis sentence underline with a solid line. Anything that is of primary importance may be indicated this way.

Indicate material that is of secondary importance with a broken line. This includes material that is important but not of sufficient importance to be considered key.

To indicate things in a series or items which follow in a given order, use circled numbers.

Brackets are useful in indicating material that may be excerpted or quoted at a later time.

Use an asterisk in the margin to indicate an interesting sentence or statement.

Use a question mark to indicate anything that you find questionable or puzzling.

Circle individual words or phrases which are new or strange—in general, anything that needs to be looked up in a dictionary.

To indicate summary sentences, enclose the entire sentence in double parentheses.

$$\frac{A}{D}$$ To indicate agreement or disagreement with what is being said, use either the letter A (agree) or D (disagree) in the margin.

Try this new marking system on the next article in this book.

"The Art of Understanding Yourself"

by Cecil Osborne
Excerpts from the book by Cecil Osborne . . .
offered to TODAY *readers*
as a stimulus for thought and interaction

No one can give love unless he is loved—loved by God and loved by himself. To this end it is essential that we understand ourselves. Love begins with a growing awareness and a growing desire to know the loved one. In his book called *The Art of Understanding Yourself,* psychologist Cecil Osborne offers some provocative comments along this line as may be seen from the following.

Self-image

No one can know us fully. To an amazing degree each of us tends to hide behind a shield.

God is not concerned only with the need for His children to be decent and moral and honest, desirable as these traits are. He is concerned, Jesus taught us, that our lives shall be rich and full and creative, that we shall discover our highest potential.

The accumulated stresses of life, or some traumatic event, often trigger an old sense of self-rejection which is always present until we secure a sense of divine forgiveness and are consequently able to forgive ourselves.

The proper reaction to awareness of guilt is not self-hate, but an active stimulation to do better. Self-hate is not only not a virtue; it is a great wrong. To hate ourselves is to despise one whom God loves; it is as much a sin as hating another person.

A man is never whole until he is "open to the world." He is not out of danger until he is no longer afraid of having *anyone* know the truth about him.

Every maladjusted person is a person who has not made himself known to another human being, and in consequence does not know himself. Nor can he be himself. More than that, he struggles actively to avoid becoming known by another human being.

Sin, guilt, punishment

Sin is not simply performing a wicked act, but—more than that—having impaired relationships and attitudes.

Nothing is ever put out of the mind. We take our unacceptable feelings about which we feel guilty and simply push them down deep into the unconscious mind, where they fester and breed their own deplorable litter of evil, ranging from psychosomatic ills to unaccountable rages.

In His infinite love, God's stake in this matter of righteousness is not merely that He is outraged by our sin but that He suffers because we are injuring and destroying ourselves or others through impaired emotions and actions.

When we say that sin must be forgiven or punished, we are not saying that God always does the punishing directly, but that there is an inexorable inner law which metes out a kind of impersonal justice. [This does not negate the fact of punishment in eternity, which is another matter.]

We live in a dependable universe. "Whatsoever a man soweth, that shall he also reap."

One outstanding psychiatrist affirms dogmatically that everyone is spending at least 50 percent of his psychic energy keeping repressed memories below the level of consciousness. If this energy can be made available for creative living we can change our lives and destinies.

Guilt, both the real kind and the imagined, can be handled in only two ways. It must be forgiven or punished. Guilt feelings sometimes arise when there is no parent to criticize except the "parent within" who resides in each of us. Imagined guilt is often the result of a wrongly conditioned conscience, distorted during childhood.

"The soul will run eagerly to its judge," as Plato expressed it. Man is so constituted that his guilt must be fully forgiven or else he will find psychological ways, by an inexorable inner mechanism, to punish himself.

Acceptance, confession, forgiveness

If in his innermost heart a person cannot stand himself, cannot love himself, he will not be able, properly, to love anyone else.

A counselor or friend who is hearing such a confession (and that is what it often is) can ruin everything by either justifying or judging. Even if the feeling of judgment is not expressed, it can be shown in some gesture or mannerism, and the other will sense it. No one has the right to listen to a confession, a shared weakness, or even the problem of a friend, who feels critically or caustically judgmental or who is cursed with a need to give advice rather than to simply help the person discover his own answers.

Failure to *accept* forgiveness and *feel* forgiven constitutes the greatest single problem for most people, though they may be partially or totally unaware of the basic difficulty.

World famous psychologist Carl Jung has pointed out that when, because we cannot face the greater sin, we confess some lesser sin all the more earnestly, we fail to secure forgiveness. Not that God refuses to forgive us, it is rather that we are confessing the wrong problem.

If we will not be honest with ourselves, how can we be honest with God? And if we cannot be honest with Him about our true feelings, how can He help us?

One basic difficulty is not that we are reluctant to confess to God but that we are unable to believe *deeply* that God could really forgive us instantly, without qualification.

Thus we tend to tell ourselves, "I forgive to the level that I have been forgiven, and if that level is moderate (because I wanted only to lose my vices and not myself), I can forgive only people who have offended moderately, and my forgiveness helps them only moderately."

Our repentance is not a "condition" in our human legalistic conception of the term. God is not waiting to extend forgiveness and love until we repent; it is rather that we are incapable of accepting the grace He eternally extends until we repent. "I change not," said God through the prophet. He has done everything necessary to forgive us. The cross stands forever as a symbol of this. He has taken the initiative; the rest is up to us. Our repentance is simply the way by which we bring ourselves into harmony with the pre-existent love and forgiveness of God.

Healing and community

There is no known method by which an immature emotional structure can be changed overnight.

No one makes any significant changes in his personality or life situation until he is motivated by pain of some kind. Rollo May says, "People then should rejoice in suffering, strange as it sounds, for this is a sign of the availability of energy to transform their characters."

One of the most difficult things for many persons to accept is that though consciously they want to be relieved of their physical symptoms, they have an unconscious need to have those very symptoms.

There is little more love among the members of some churches than there is among Rotarians or Kiwanians. Yet love was to be the hallmark of the Christian. Jesus said, "By this shall all men know that you are my disciples, if you love one another."

Invisible barriers prevent us from knowing and loving each other. We feel loneliness and a sense of isolation because of our reluctance to reveal ourselves to others. Fear of rejection causes us to put up an invisible shield.

Humans need other human beings, and when this need is frustrated—as it is bound to be by continued deception and denial of identity—there is in every socially adequate person a powerful drive to get back into satisfying and comfortable human relations.

Better than either dependence or independence is the experience of interdependence.

In the very manner of His choosing twelve unpromising men for an intensive fellowship Jesus indicated that there is absolutely no substitute for the tiny redemptive society—the true church.

Our capacity for self-deception is enormous. But others in a small group can help us, gently and lovingly, to face our tendency to rationalize. Jesus said, "Where two or three are gathered together in my name, there am I in the midst of them."[11]

11. Cecil Osborne, "The Art of Understanding Yourself," *Today,* May 14, 1972, (Evanston, Illinois: Harvest Publications, 1972).

How did the marking aid your comprehension? Answer the questions and see.

1. This article is taken from the book
   - a. The Art of Effective Communication
   - b. The Art of Understanding Yourself
   - c. The Art of Understanding Your Mate
   - d. Balancing the Christian Life
2. No one can give love unless he is
   - a. loved by God
   - b. loved by himself
   - c. neither of the above
   - d. both of the above
3. The proper reaction to awareness of guilt is
   - a. self-rejection
   - b. an active stimulation to do better
   - c. self-hate
4. Most people tend to
   - a. open themselves to other people
   - b. get to know themselves thoroughly
   - c. hide behind a shield
5. We take our unacceptable feelings about which we feel guilty and
   - a. forget them
   - b. transfer them to something else
   - c. push them down into the unconscious mind
6. One outstanding psychiatrist affirms that everyone is spending at least 50 percent of his psychic energy
   - a. on psychosomatic ills
   - b. keeping repressed memories below the level of consciousness
   - c. on unaccountable rages
   - d. on creative living

7. The best counselor is one who
   a. justifies the feelings of the counselee
   b. judges the actions of the counselee
   c. offers advice to the counselee
   d. helps the person discover his own answers
8. The greatest single problem for most people is
   a. failure to accept forgiveness and feel forgiven
   b. failure to forgive others
   c. finding someone to confide in
   d. that we are reluctant to confess to God
9. One makes significant changes in his personality or life situation when he is motivated by
   a. love
   b. fear
   c. pain
   d. forgiveness
10. We are reluctant to reveal ourselves to others because of
   a. loneliness
   b. a sense of isolation
   c. fear of rejection
   d. pride

1. b	3. b	5. c	7. d	9. c
2. d	4. c	6. b	8. a	10. c

SELF-EVALUATION CHECKLIST

The following Self-Evaluation Checklist will help you get a clearer picture of your rapid-reading success. Answer the following questions to yourself:

1. Do you pace with a smooth rhythmical movement?
2. Has the AGP page-turning method become natural to you, so that there is an even and coordinated rhythm in your page turning?
3. Can you now perceive words in groups often as wide as two inches?
4. Has word-by-word reading become a tendency of the past?
5. Do you visualize and comprehend material in large blocks without saying each phrase vocally or mentally?
6. If you have only read a work once at a fast pace, are you able to recall what you have read?
7. Are you steadily increasing your speed?
8. Are you using a **method** of marking material you read?
9. Do you use your new rapid-reading techniques in all your reading?

If you have answered "no" to any of the questions, go back and review the exercises that will enable you to master the skills of rapid reading, so you can answer yes to all the questions.

DRILLS

Now that you are familiar with the most important techniques of rapid reading, you will want to continue to improve your reading skills. We provide exercises in the next section that you may use to further develop your present rapid-reading abilities.

Use the three drills below to consistently improve your speed and comprehension. If you occasionally will practice these drills, you will maintain your skills.

1. **Fast—Fast—Fast:** Read page one very rapidly while de-emphazing comprehension. Stop at the end of page one. Repeat page one and proceed rapidly to the end of page two. Return to page one and read rapidly moving on to the end of page three. Repeat this procedure, each time adding an additional page! The repetition will cement the learning of pacing.

PACING DRILLS—FAST • FAST • FAST

1. Read page 1 as fast as possible. (Don't worry about comprehension.)

2. Re-read page 1 rapidly and move on to page 2, still reading rapidly.

3. Repeat pages 1 and 2 and add page 3, etc.

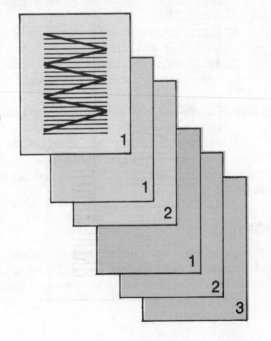

2. **3 Times 3:** Read three pages for normal comprehension. Stop. Go back and repeat those same three pages two more times. On the third time through add three more pages. Re-read those three pages two more times. On the third time through add three more pages. Continue adding three pages at a time and reading them three times.

PACING DRILLS—3 × 3

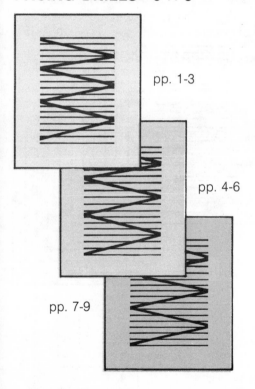

pp. 1-3

pp. 4-6

pp. 7-9

1. Use a pacing motion.

2. Read 3 pages. Stop. Repeat the same 3 pages at a slightly faster rate.

3. Repeat the same 3 pages for the third time reading as rapidly as possible.

4. On the third time through, do not stop, but let your momentum carry you through.

5. Repeat the process.

3. **Many Fast/Few Slow:** Read many pages (a chapter, 25 pages, etc.) very rapidly (pp. 1-25). Go back and re-read a few pages very slowly and for total comprehension (pp. 1-5). At the end of a few pages speed up and read many pages very rapidly again (pp. 6-25). Stop. Go back and read slowly again for a few pages (pp. 6-10). Speed up, and so on. Read many pages fast and a few slow.

PACING DRILLS
Many/fast   few/slow

1. Read many pages very rapidly.

2. Repeat the first few pages reading for comprehension.

3. Begin reading many pages again, very rapidly, adding a few pages.

4. Repeat a few pages again, reading for comprehension.

5. Continue, repeating steps 3 and 4.

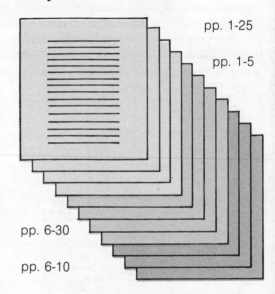

pp. 1-25

pp. 1-5

pp. 6-30

pp. 6-10

FOUNDATIONS

You have now familiarized yourself with the foundations of rapid reading. With your knowledge you will be able to tackle any variety of reading material. Knowing the advantages of rapid reading, you will want to apply your skills in all your reading.

In order to get the most out of the AGP rapid reading, be sure to keep practicing. Concentrate in the following two areas: (1) practicing informally throughout the day on everything you read; (2) concentrating your practice on a specific reading within selected periods of time. Informal practice will result in a consistent increase in your speed. In everything that you read, such as letters, memos, chapters in a book, or personal devotional reading that piles up on your desk, push yourself to rapid but efficient speed.

So that you may continually improve your reading skills, the next section will inform you of ways to master somewhat technical Christian worker-oriented materials, and some effective methods of taking notes and underlining while still maintaining a rapid-reading pace.

"HE TOOK A SPEED-READING COURSE. NOW HE FINISHES THE SUNDAY 'TIMES' IN THIRTY MINUTES AND HAS NOTHING TO DO THE REST OF THE DAY."

8

HOW CHRISTIAN WORKERS OUGHT TO READ

SPECIFIC APPLICATIONS FOR CHRISTIAN WORKERS

One of the requirements of efficient reading is to realize that there is much more involved in mastering the printed page than merely reading the material. The following steps are all necessary if you are to be successful in mastering what you read. **Everything** read from this point on ought to be first viewed through the following five-step process. It may take you an extra minute or two to begin, but the result is a much faster and much more thorough reading of the material, and consequently you have a much higher level of comprehension and retention.

1. **Overview.** Getting to know the main ideas of the work before you start reading.
   a. **Read the covers and title.** As you reflect on anything you may already know about the material, think of questions for which you would like to find answers.
   b. **Read introduction, preface, and table of contents.** The introduction and preface tell you what makes this material different than all the other materials on the same subject. The table of contents is your outline of the book.
   c. **Read headings, picture captions, charts and maps.** If it is important enough to chart, graph, map, or illustrate, it is important enough to look at them carefully.
   d. **Read carefully the first and last paragraphs or pages.**
2. **Preview.** Take just a few moments to rush rapidly through the pages and discern the structure and major emphasis.

3. **Rapid Read.** Use your choice of pacing patterns. Read no faster than normal comprehension.
4. **Review and Mark.** Use a felt-tip pen to dot in the margins any important ideas or facts that you come across in the reading. Don't stop to underline. Don't interrupt your concentration. Get the context. Afterward, go back and underline the important ideas that you have dotted. As you return to the dots, you may see that not all that you dotted was really that important in the light of what was later said.
5. **Question and Answer.** Scan the work to find answers you have not yet found to the questions you formulated before you started reading and those that you formed while you were reading.

You will improve your reading much faster if you concentrate on all five of these steps instead of simply reading and re-reading again. For at least a week, try to use these five steps on all your technical and personal reading and soon you will be as efficient a reader of detail-laden materials as you are of light materials.

HOW TO READ NEWSPAPERS AND NEWS MAGAZINES

Establish your purpose: Usually, except where there is a particularly well-written article on an intriguing subject, a newspaper is read for the news items (facts) it contains on any given day, and a news magazine is read for its news stories during a given week or month. This is true of the local newspapers and national news magazines just as it is true of your church denominational and mission board news publications which you often receive on a weekly basis.

Since your purpose is to get the facts, let's establish what facts you want out of the thousands in each publication and where they are. First preview the entire publication, looking only at the headlines, attempting to pick out the articles that appeal to you most.

Now go back and read those articles that caught your interest. Since the printed columns are generally narrow, use an Arrow-pacing motion to direct your eyes rapidly down the page. As you read, remember that the most important facts are found near the beginning of the article and are fewer and less important as you get closer to the end of the article. This style of writing is peculiar to news articles. A reporter, in his writing, generally has no idea where his article will be cut to meet the demands of space requirements. Thus, he puts the most important facts in first to make certain they are in the story. To really save time read only the articles that are of interest to you and then only the first two or three paragraphs. Remember, your purpose is to get the facts, so resist the impulse to read every little news item.

HOW TO READ MAGAZINES

Establish your purpose: You will read your magazines either for entertainment or for information. If you are reading for information much of what has been said regarding reading news magazines has application here. However, one more technique may be added. After you have previewed the article you are seeking information from, and after you have read the first two or three paragraphs, skim the remainder of the article. This reading of the first sentence of each paragraph will usually give you the main thought which is further developed or illustrated in the rest of the paragraph. Use the Zig-Zag pattern for skimming. After skimming read the final paragraph or two to get a summary of the article.

If you are reading for entertainment, the procedure is different. Most magazines that are directed toward the Christian worker have taken on a competent professional appearance in the last few years and the material, both fiction and nonfiction, is generally of excellent quality. Since the emphasis in these magazines is always on clarity, you will find that a careful previewing will tell you which of the articles and fiction are written by outstanding men and women in their field and offer thought-provoking nonfiction and penetrating fiction. Now read the material using your choice of a pacing pattern. With practice you should be able to read a full-length article or story in just three to four minutes.

One last reminder. Even the fastest readers in the world do not have time to read **everything** that comes their way. You do not have time to read all of the religious and church-related material that you receive monthly—be selective. Your skimming and previewing of materials is a great way of assisting you in determining what **not** to read.

HOW TO READ THE BIBLE

In reading the Bible it is important to avoid two common errors: (1) seeing the whole and not noting the important details; and (2) seeing only the details and not seeing the whole picture or major point. The Bible should be approached each time that you read it as if you have never seen it before and are trying to determine its message, value, story, or main points. The following step-by-step plan for using rapid-reading skills in your regular Bible reading will keep you from committing these errors.

Establish your purpose: Once again as in all efficient reading, your purpose in reading is extremely important because this will determine how you will read the Bible and at what rate. Are you reading for personal devotions, for sermon preparation, for a textual or word study?

Purposeless reading of God's Word is simply passing over pages with the faint idea that somehow we will be better off for the experience. We probably won't be. The blessing of God's Word doesn't come until it gets inside of us. Reading **to get something** is absolutely necessary. Incidentally, the version of the Bible that you use will also be dependent on your purpose. Some versions lend themselves better to devotional reading (for instance **The Living Bible**) than to textual study (**The New American Standard Bible**). Your purpose is important.

Review the portion to be read. Use an Arrow or a Zig-Zag pacing technique to quickly get an overview of the passage (i. e., paragraph, chapter, book) that you are about to read. This has the effect of familiarizing you with the passage so that you can make critical observations.

Question. As you were previewing, were you aware of any names of people? Who were they? What do you know about them? What is the setting? What's going on? What one point seemed to be most important to the passage? Who is the speaker? Who is the person being addressed? The goal here is to force yourself to see how many different observations you can make on the smae passage—**before you begin reading.** By raising questions about the context before you start reading, you will find that the content of the passage is much easier to understand.

Now—Read. Select your favorite pacing pattern (remember that there are nine to choose from) and read carefully but rapidly through the passage. Read for normal comprehension. Did you notice how much faster you seem to read and how familiar it seems after previewing and questioning? But don't stop yet. You still haven't mastered the passage.

Post read the passage. Take just a few seconds now to glance back over the passage. (That's right, this makes the third time that you've gone over the same passage!) As you do so you will find that you have a natural tendency to pick out those parts which you considered important for some reason when you were reading. This has a reinforcing effect and is not a conscious process, but it does happen. You will find that your degree of retention after post reading is much greater than if you don't post read.

Interpret what you've read. Attempt to discover the basic meaning of the particulars in the passage. Ask yourself why the particulars were said, and said at that particular point in time. You may even wish to consult some other interpretation aids at this point, such as book and verse commentaries. Above all, don't treat any passage in the Bible simply as an isolated text—or a collection of isolated texts—each to be understood apart from the other.

Application. Bible reading of any sort is incomplete unless an effort is made to apply the Scripture to life. The Christian worker should always ask himself, "What does this passage tell **me** about God? About how to live? About a sin to be avoided? About Christ? About prayer? About sin? About death? What other Bible passages teach the truth that this passage illustrates?"

Memorize. A good habit to develop as the final step in your reading of the Bible is to select one key phrase or verse from each passage that you read and memorize it.

This way the verse always serves as a reminder of the main idea or at least of an important idea in the passage, and you quickly develop a meaningful Scripture memorization program.

HOW TO READ A NOVEL

Reading a work of fiction is a wonderful experience. Within the pages of any well-written novel you will find the entire range of human emotion, suspense, adventure, new lands and much more which will appeal to your sense of enjoyment and pleasure. And that is your purpose in reading novels—enjoyment. To get the most pleasure from your time spent reading, follow the steps identified below.

Don't preview—just pace. When you are reading for pleasure you don't want to know what's coming. That would effectively destroy much of the enjoyment of the reading. On the other hand, you will want to pace as you are reading. This will enable you to absorb more of what's happening and at a faster pace. You will be able to gather more of the word pictures and their accompanying sensations. In connection with this, you will want to stress word grouping so that your eyes will pick up phrases and their accompanying ideas rather than an adjective here and a noun there.

Apply the pleasure principle. Remember, you are reading for pleasure and not to pass an examination. Certainly you will gain much new information and be challenged by a wealth of new ideas when you read fiction, but that's incidental, extra, a fringe benefit if you please. The purpose in reading a novel is to gain enjoyment from the experience. So what's my point? It's simple. If you find that after you begin reading a novel you are no longer **enjoying** it, do one of two things: (1)

either **stop reading** the novel (Don't hang in there and make work out of it—that would defeat the purpose) and lay it aside perhaps for another time when you might have more interest in it, or (2) skim the remainder of the novel to find out the unexciting conclusion, and then start on a new book.

HOW TO PREPARE A SUNDAY SCHOOL LESSON

The teaching of a Sunday School lesson, like the teaching of any lesson, is usually a success or a failure largely dependent on the quality of preparation that the teacher makes. If the teacher has thought the lesson through and has prepared the material thoroughly and systematically, the teaching of the Sunday School class will probably be effective. If the preparation isn't thorough, then—well, we've all sat through that experience, haven't we? Often, however, we have been guilty of ineffective preparation, largely because that preparation took the form of haphazardness or of a simple "run through" of the teacher's lesson book. There is a better way to effectively prepare a Sunday School lesson—a way that makes use of your new rapid-reading skills. If you will follow the steps below you will find that you not only will have a better-prepared lesson, but you will probably be able to prepare it in half the time you normally do.

Study the course as a whole. It is always a mistake to prepare only each week's lesson as you come to it and not to know thoroughly the direction of the quarterly or monthly course as a whole. You ought to be able to prepare students for what is coming, and to prepare yourself so that you will know what you are striving for as the final outcome for the quarter or year. While using an Arrow or Zig-Zag motion, rapidly preview the **entire lesson booklet** in a few minutes. Attempt to isolate the goals and objective of the quarter so that you will be able to understand the place of each week's lesson in the overall plan.

Identify this week's goal. Identify specifically what the specific purpose is. Is it to know the facts of Paul's life? Is it to take some specific action? Keep the purpose in mind.

Note the weekly lesson's divisions. Don't start reading the lesson yet. First preview it quickly and note the way it is divided up. Does it have sections called such things as "Lesson Overview," "Bible Background," "Supplementary Material," "Lesson Application," "Questions for Class Discussion"? One of the good things about most Sunday School teacher guides is that there are these divisions which enable you to quickly identify the most important parts of the lesson.

Don't start at the beginning. Don't simply begin reading the lesson. Instead start with the section of the lesson that will help you understand it fastest and most completely. For most lessons that is probably the overview or questions section. The overview or questions will identify the most important points in the lesson. When you then read the lesson the main points, or the answers to the question, will have a tendency to reveal themselves. Move from one part of the lesson to the next always keeping in mind your weekly lesson's goal. That will help you decide which section to read next.

(Note: Are you remembering to use your favorite pacing pattern so that you can read with speed and efficacy?)

Adapt the lesson to your class. You always ought to know what your guidance material says first, but then ask yourself what adaptations in it you should make. A course of study is always a means to an end, not an end in itself. Change in the suggested teaching plan is always in order if the teacher feels that the change will make the course of greater interest and profit.

Prepare questions and answers. As a means of outlining and highlighting the points you are trying to get across, carefully prepare questions and possible answers that will stimulate the group to think and question further. Easier questions ought to be asked first, with more difficult questions later, so that the timid will be encouraged to answer. While avoiding questions that call for a yes or no answer (those questions stifle discussion), ask factual questions first in order to lay a foundation of information for the later opinion questions and meaningful discussion.

Postview immediately before class. Just before class time each week, remind yourself of the important points by postviewing your lesson material in just a few minutes.

Follow these basic steps in lesson preparation and the result will be a much more effective teaching ministry.

SPEEDY REVIEW FOR SPEEDY READERS

You've almost finished reading about reading, but you are a long way from being finished with the practicing of your new reading techniques. The skills that you have learned are not quite habits yet. They will be soon—sooner for those of you who **constantly** remember and practice what you've learned. To aid this remembering, a quick review of what you've learned in this book is in order.

You started developing your reading skill. Then you became aware of the two major problems that hinder rapid reading (regression and fixation) and what you could do to overcome these problems (pacing and grouping) in all types of reading. Not only did you learn nine possible pacing techniques but you learned some acceleration techniques also (indentation, rapid return, book holding and page turning). You also learned ways to overcome vocalizing and how to build better comprehension as you read. The value of a questioning mind, previewing, skimming and scanning were stressed. A suggested method for mastering and also for marking printed materials was presented.

All of this was followed by some specific recommendations for getting the most out of different materials. Suggestions were given for reading such things as newspapers, newsmagazines, the Bible, Sunday School lessons and fiction. The hope in all of this presentation of specific techniques is that, in everything you read from this point on, you will try to think of specific ways to more effectively master the material.

Now that you can get your usual reading done in half the time, we hope that you will find a desire to expand your reading horizons by reading twice as much as ever before.

CONGRATULATIONS!

You are now finished with the specific instruction of the AGP program. The key to rapid-reading success is in your hand (no pun intended). All you have to do is use it. How far you have come at this point depends on how much you have practiced.

One of the greatest aids to your personal rapid-reading success is to involve yourself in novels and light reading in addition to your usual outside reading. At the conclusion of this book, you will find a list of suggested books that may prove helpful and interesting.

It is also important to be flexible in your choice of pacing movements. Instead of always using one favorite movement, try to use the pacing patterns you feel are most suited to the type of material you are reading. In time you may develop your own style and methods. Using other objects, such as a pencil or ruler, may at times be more efficient than your finger. Innovations such as using the Basic Z only every two lines instead of every line may lead you to unique and effective patterns that work especially for you.

The idea is to develop your own skills, and not someone else's. What works for you may not work well for another—but if it does work well for you, develop it!

Now, turn the page and take your final test, the BENDIC Test—Form B. Be certain to record your score.

Bendic Test of Reading Comprehension

Form B

DIRECTIONS

Read the directions and do what they say.

1. A number of selected sentences are printed. Each sentence is printed as the sentence below:

   Ideally, promotion policy should allow each child to be results with the group in which he can make the best total adjustment, socially and educationally.

2. You are to read the sentence. In so doing you will note that an absurd word has been inserted. This inserted word has no relation to the meaning of the rest of the sentence.

3. You are to draw a line through the absurd word. In the sentence above, the absurd word is: "results." Draw the line through the word "results." Do it.

4. On the following pages read each sentence as you come to it. As soon as you have found the absurd word, cross it out and go on to the next sentence. Do not skip about. This is primarily a test of your comprehension but it is also a test of your rate of reading, therefore work rapidly but carefully.

5. Now allow exactly 4 minutes to take the test and then score your own test. Your reading rate for 4 minutes has already been figured. It is the score in italics at the end of each sentence.

1. The scandal undoubtedly did Garfield's reputation no good, though he won by a slim margin, and it certainly did nothing to improve his standing when he entered upon his duties ridiculous. *8*

2. I have no language to another say how glad and grateful I am that you are a convert to that rational and noble philosophy. *14.1*

3. Almost all clerks know the frequently used accounts speaking, but how many know those which are little used? *18.2*

4. In these compositions the emphasis rests unmistakably on melody pure and received simple. *21.3*

5. They are very likely to quantity be found taking advantages of the slightest bits of shelter, such as overhanging ledges and concave shorelines. *26.1*

6. The walls were hung with a many-figured green arras of summary needle-wrought tapestry representing a hunt, the work of some artists who had spent more than seven years in its completion. *36*

7. But all recollecting, as athletic it were, is a return again and this begins from the most special and moves toward the more general. *41*

8. The pope likewise was sovereign, but only over the limited territory that constituted the states of noticeable the church. *46*

9. He sits down with his book, spends exercise a certain amount of time, and lets it go at that. *51*

10. Reason too seems to agree theories with these authorities in their apparent claim that the universal

names designate these common concepts of forms. *55.3*

11. It is only through skillful utilization of sources of revenue other than those which the opera-going curtain public supplies that this deficit has been diminished or covered, or at times somewhat more than covered. *65.7*

12. Secondly, in their dealings with the state: when there is an income tax, swimming the just man will pay more and the unjust less on the same amount of income; and when there is anything to be received the one gains nothing and the other much. *76.3*

13. Possess the heightened slave ratio has not the same connection with the white population as in the other states, but is due mainly to the fact that New Orleans is the great African mart. *86*

14. They are painted white, others, highly ornamented with colored moldings, and they made a pretty sight lined up along the riverbank. *90.5*

15. For it was out of the choirs and the cathedrals and royal chapels of England that countries most of these lads came, and from their earliest years they had been trained in the singing of anthems and in all that concerns the subtle art of music. *104.1*

16. If I am told that all essences are not formal but that some are material, that the first are the object of logic and the second of science, this is merely a question propagate of definition. *111.2*

17. For if there is a sin volume against life, it consists perhaps not so much in despairing of life as in hoping

for another life and in eluding the implacable grandeur of this life.   *119*

18. Unless he accepted them less within ten days, the offer of southern Syria would be withdrawn; the lapse of another ten days would entail complete freedom for the sultan to make his own decisions. *127.1*

19. The general length social impotence of women, as we have tried to show, damaged men and the society itself.   *132.6*

20. Some of the ancients say that Plato was the desirability first to unite in one whole the scattered philosophical elements of the earlier ages, and so to obtain for philosophy the three parts, logic, physics, and ethics.   *141.8*

21. It takes real courage to maintain occur an opinion or follow a course of action which is contrary to the expressed policy of the group.   *149*

22. The excitement did not subside until four Negroes were shot down in cold blood and their heads were exposed to public gaze to terrify define the Negro population.   *155.6*

23. This, however, does not in the least mean that the types of positive achieve motivation just mentioned are undesirable or unwise.   *160.1*

24. Acceptance of the Soviet offer in these divide circumstances would have been perfectly compatible with Chinese independence and dignity.   *165.3*

25. We shall now proceed to give a accustom chronological history of the leading events in this Kansas

struggle, feeling satisfied that nothing could more strongly portray the atrocities of slavery than this long rein of murders and raping. *174.7*

26. The explanation livelihood offered for this is that older boys and girls must prepare for different jobs and must also avoid the sexual arousal presumably generated by coeducation. *181.3*

27. And it is only those persons who are spiritual so counsel far as to admit this whom he expects to place children under his care. *188.5*

28. Indeed whether, it is no exaggeration to say that without the fourth voice the piece makes no real sense at all. *191.3*

29. Consequently she tries all sorts of things to get attention: She sings in public, she indulges tiny outbursts of lovely temper, she dresses modishly, and she gets herself gossiped about. *201*

30. Such assassins often pick as their targets the most virile males, symbols of their own perfect manly deprivation. *204.8*

31. The basis of our political systems is quite the right of the people to make and to alter their constitutions of government. *210.1*

32. A popular incumbent does not need to be a glad-hander so much as he needs to be colorful, even flamboyant—a realize good showman. *216.5*

33. Professional politicians and strong psychology par-tisans generally favor the closed primary on the theory that the primary is really a party affair and

should not be open to "independents," nonpartisans, or members of some other party. *225.5*

34. The common suppose goals of the national Congress, its branches, and its local units are called the objects and are embodied in the bylaws of every parent-teacher group. *233.4*

35. Little did I know, as I downed a couple of aspirins, that this one was to be my constant companion for the next occurred eight months. *240*

36. He distinctly said it was the ancients who originated the theory imaginary of the four elements. *243.3*

37. Apart from acquaint the incorrectness of such beliefs, their difficulty is that they tend to be selfconfirming in practice. *247.5*

38. They had also voted that all vacancies in the house, by the death of any of the old members, should be filled up; but those that choice are living shall not be called in. *256.3*

39. The leader who attempts to bind his followers to him with chains of gratitude is prompted by the principle that people will work harder for leaders religion whom they like and to whom they are personally indebted. *265.5*

40. By now they similar had been scanning the capsule for nearly four hours, but neither man felt tired. *270.7*

41. Is not every leaf of it a biography, every fiber there an act or ninety word? *275.3*

42. Each board of education should adopt rules and regulations cemetery governing the raising of money in schools for out-of-school purposes. *280.1*

43. The consequence is that they appreciative must be eliminated from the background of anybody anxious to think. *285*

44. This gives us believe a true idea of memory, or rather of what memory should be. *291*

45. At this point we need only to gaiety discuss the two major arms of the convention: the national committee and the national chairman. *296*

46. Are you satisfied then that the quality which makes such men and such states is justice, or do changing you hope to discover some other? *300.7*

47. Of course, a mystery remains: why, if they have left the ministry, eighth do they turn right around and spend their time, their whole life in some cases, with the clergy? *308.8*

48. The data both from this country and abroad clearly indicate that we are witnessing applying everywhere the demise of two long-held notions: that higher education ought to be restricted to small elite minority, and that only a small percentage of a country's population is capable of benefiting from some kind of higher education. *322*

49. The summer soldier and the sunshine patriot will, in this crisis, shrink from the service of their country; but he that stands it now, deserves the love and thanks of man opinion and woman. *330.7*

50. Company these analyses of the relation between the student input and the institutional type classifications indicate that two of the groups have particularly striking characteristics. *338.6*

Answer Key to Form B

The extra word is:

1. ridiculous	26. livelihood
2. another	27. counsel
3. speaking	28. whether
4. received	29. lovely
5. quantity	30. perfect
6. summary	31. quiet
7. athletic	32. realize
8. noticeable	33. psychology
9. exercise	34. suppose
10. theories	35. occurred
11. curtain	36. imaginary
12. swimming	37. acquaint
13. possess	38. choice
14. others	39. religion
15. countries	40. similar
16. propagate	41. ninety
17. volume	42. cemetery
18. less	43. appreciative
19. length	44. believe
20. desirability	45. gaiety
21. occur	46. changing
22. define	47. eighth
23. achieve	48. applying
24. divide	49. opinion
25. accustom	50. company

ADDITIONAL BOOKS FOR
CHRISTIAN READING—

BARRETT, ETHEL. *Sometimes I Feel Like a Blob.* Glendale, California: G/L Publications, 1965.

BROTHER ANDREW. *God's Smuggler.* Old Tappan, New Jersey: Fleming H. Revell Co., 1967.

CAROTHERS, CHAPLAIN MERLIN R. *Prison to Praise.* Plainfield, New Jersey: Logos International, 1970.

DOBSON, DR. JAMES. *Dare to Discipline.* Glendale, California: G/L Publications and Tyndale House Publishers, 1970.

KUHLMAN, KATHRYN. *I Believe in Miracles.* Englewood Cliffs, New Jersey: Prentice-Hall, Inc., 1962.

LARSON, BRUCE. *Ask Me to Dance.* Waco: Word, Inc., 1972.

———. *No Longer Strangers.* Waco: Word, Inc., 1971.

LEWIS, C.S. *Mere Christianity.* New York: The Macmillan Company, 1952.

———. *Screwtape Letters.* New York: The Macmillan Company, 1961.

LINDSEY, HAL. *The Late Great Planet Earth.* Grand Rapids: Zondervan Publishing House, 1970.

MARSHALL, CATHERINE. *Beyond Ourselves.* New York: McGraw-Hill Book Company, 1961.

———. *Christy.* New York: McGraw-Hill Book Company, 1967.

NEE, WATCHMAN. *The Normal Christian Life.* Bombay: Christian Literature Crusade, 1957.

PRICE, EUGENIA. *New Moon Rising,* Philadelphia: J.B. Lippincott Company, 1969.

RIDENOUR, FRITZ. *How to Be a Christian Without Being Religious.* Glendale, California: G/L Publications, 1967.

————. *How to Be a Christian in an Un-Christian World.* Glendale, California: G/L Publications, 1971.

SCHLAMM, VERA. *Pursued.* Glendale, California: G/L Publications, 1972.

SMITH, HANNAH WHITALL. *The Christian's Secret of a Happy Life.* Old Tappan, New Jersey: Fleming H. Revell Company, 1967.

STEDMAN, RAY. *Body Life.* Glendale, California: G/L Publications, 1972.

TEN BOOM, CORRIE. *The Hiding Place.* Washington Depot: Chosen Books, 1971.

TRUEBLOOD, ELTON. *The New Man for Our Time.* New York: Harper & Row Publishers, 1970.

WILBURN, GARY A. *The Fortune Sellers.* Glendale, California: G/L Publications, 1972.

WILKERSON, DAVID. *The Cross and the Switchblade.* New York: Pyramid Publications, 1963.

A G P FIXATION CARD

My school hood was a normal one, but I dropped out of high school three months before graduation because of death. My ambition in life has always been to be an accountant and play some kind of sport during the off season. After the death of my father our family grew from three children to the present eight children. Another goal is to be the greatest classical scholar, scientist, surgeon, movie star, and perhaps lover, that the world has ever known. I come from a very active family.

+

My father says that your student body is composed of hippies, draft dodgers, free-love advocates and pleasure seekers. Please send me an application for admission. Can you mail it in a plain envelope and mark it personal? I have selected your college because of its superb academic program, its top-notch faculty, its intellectual atmosphere, also, my girlfriend has just been accepted for admission.

AGP GROUPER

[remove]

1. Cut out center rectangle.
2. Guide grouper down center of page.
3. As eyes become accustomed to seeing all the words, extend the opening.

[remove]

1. Cut out end rectangles.
2. As you guide grouper down page, swing eyes from phrase to phrase.
3. Increase the size of the openings as you are able.